MW00831353

COVID -19
"MEET MY GOD"

(Faith Over Fear)

MARY ANN WILSON

LEGAL DISCLAIMER

This book is designed to provide information and motivation to my readers. It is sold with the understanding the author is not engaged to render any type of psychological or any other kind of professional advice. The content is the sole expression and opinion of the author. The author shall not be liable for any psychological, emotional, financial, or commercial damages, including, but not limited to special, incidental, consequential or other damages. You are responsible for your own choices, actions and results.

COVID -19 MEET MY GOD
Copyright © 2020 Mary Ann Wilson

Printed in the United States of America

ISBN: 978-0-578-81696-8

Dedication

This book is dedicated to all COVID-19 survivors, those currently infected and those mourning the loss of family members due to COVID-19. This virus has taken away many loved ones throughout the world, leaving families devastated from the loss. This book is a dedicated memorial for those who died alone in a hospital room without the presence of family and friends. For those who are presently struggling with this virus, this book is a testimonial to help you tap into a survivor's instead of a victim's mentality by believing in God, your higher power source, knowing God can heal you when you choose faith over fear.

To my mother, Evelyn Hollins, the matriarch of our family, I could not have made it this far in my life without your example of courage and your teachings on how to lean on our heavenly father when there is no one else to lean on. Thank You for your strength and for helping me understand our experience with COVID-19 was "just a little wind" and not the feared death sentence it could have been. God blessed our family with healing and another opportunity to fulfill our God-given purpose.

To my Father God, my power source, this book is a testimonial of Your power and presence in my life. It is an edification of how You will carry your children when they cannot carry themselves. It was during my darkest moments. You became my light when I could not see my way through healing from COVID-19. My God, it was You who removed my fear of dying and losing my family members to COVID-19. God, this book is my Hallelujah to You for gifting me the courage to confront, overcome the Goliath of the giant by introducing COVID-19 to You, my power source.

Table of Contents

Introduction

A s the death tolls continue to rise throughout the world from this COVID-19 pandemic, I decided to write a book to share my family's experience while being infected by this highly contagious disease. I share how we overcame our fear by tapping into our faith, trusting God to bring us through this experience alive. Ten members of my family were infected during the same time frame. We lived in four different households. We were all infected, becoming ill around the same time. Our ages ranged from 20 to 75.

When the virus began to spread throughout the United States in March 2020, I felt like the rug was pulled from under us. It was a difficult, stressful time going to work, shopping, being separated from family members, and living in quarantine. As a therapist, I worked in a psychiatric hospital providing daily mental health group sessions, teaching coping skills to adult patients. I was considered an essential worker. I worked at the beginning of the shutdown for three months until I became overwhelmed, burnt out and subsequently resigned from my job. I am a single empty nester. I live alone. I feared what would happen if I became infected by the virus.

The death rate statistics for the African American community looked bleak. I was afraid I would die if I contracted the disease because of having an underlying medical condition, which reportedly placed me at high risk of developing severe complications from the virus.

Writing this book is a testimonial of how my faith and trust in God became the prominent focus of my healing from COVID-19. I overcame my fear of dying by trusting God to carry me through to healing. My faith was stretched and tested. I trusted God more during the time I was sick with the virus than I can remember throughout my lifetime. God did it. He came through for my family and me. I was transformed. I began a closer daily walk with Him.

I will share my personal as well as the experience of my family members while being infected with COVID-19. My desire is to encourage faith over fear, share hope to let my readers know with God we can be victorious in any crisis we may encounter. My testimony of healing is to spread the good news about the power of prayer and how God's presence made the difference in my and my family's lives. We never could have made it without God.

Dealing with a crisis can create fear and uncertainties. COVID-19 is a novel virus terrorizing many people throughout the world. The impact has been monumental and substantive. Over one million people have lost their lives due to complications posed on the immune system where they were unable to survive the attacks from the virus. The virus is unpredictable. No one really knows what impact it will have on a person's body. There are common documented symptoms, but the impact on the immune system is different for each person. Members of my family had different responses. I will share our personal experiences of how we overcame this crisis with God.

Part 1 outlines my personal account of my family's experience while sick with COVID-19. I will also share coping strategies to use to manage stress and anxiety to facilitate healing while fighting the virus.

Part 11 outlines some of the changes and impacts we have faced as a result of this unprecedented pandemic. I will also share coping strategies to help maintain our sanity while being isolated and/or quarantined during this pandemic.

Part 1
My Family's Personal Experience with COVID-19

God is our refuge and strength, a very present help in troubles. Psalm 46:1

Chapter 1
The beginning of COVID-19 Exposure

Spending time with my family in Eufaula has been one of my most enjoyable experiences since moving away over 20 years ago. My visit with my family in August 2020 was no different. I cherish seeing my 75 years old mother and other family members. I enjoy the delicious southern home-cooked meals making memories with them. I did not realize until days after the visit, I had been exposed to the virus while visiting my family's home. My family members did not know they had been exposed and infected with the virus until days after the initial contact.

They are uncertain where they made initial contact with being exposed to the virus. They suspect contact was made when my mother cared for a sick relative who lives in a different home. My mother started complaining of sinus drainage and stomach issues after she had visited her relative. My mother went to the emergency on a Sunday with a temperature of 104, was taken to the x-ray department to explore her chest and facial areas, diagnosed with sinus problems, given a shot for nausea, antibiotics, and sent home.

She stated she felt better after taking the shot and antibiotics. She returned home from the emergency department and started with her cooking routine for Sunday dinner. She loves to cook, feed her family and community. Her family, friends and senior citizens in the community loves to eat her good soul foods. It is her ministry to cook to feed the elders, her friends and family members. She always says, "I cook with love." In fact, her cooking and feeding her community is an act of love.

She is a Christian woman who believes in sharing her calling of serving others. She believes in giving and helping others. Even as a child, I remember her cooking and feeding people in our community. I also have never seen her food pantry empty. God has always multiplied what she has given out. It is called sowing good seeds and reaping a good harvest.

On August 23, 2020, I traveled from my home in Montgomery, Alabama, to Eufaula, Alabama, which is a one and a half hour's drive. I reached Eufaula around 3pm the same Sunday my mother had gone to the local emergency department, was treated and returned home. As I entered my mother's home, I could smell the aroma of soul food already cooked. She and my nephew had already prepared plates for someone to pick up.

However, that person never came for the plates that day. Meanwhile, I was questioning my mother about her emergency room visit. I asked if she had been tested for COVID 19 since she stated her temperature was 104 when she entered the emergency department at the local hospital. She stated she was informed by Emergency staff she did not need a test for the virus since the x-ray showed she had a sinus infection and was treated for it. I am a social worker by profession, and my intuitions kicked in. I felt uneasy spending the night at my mother's house because I was concerned about her not having been tested for the virus. She tried to assure me she was ok and did not have COVID-19.

I laid down my concerns, was overtaken by the smell of my mother's good food. I did not resist the urge to eat some of it. I prayed over my food as usual. I ate up her delicious cooking as usual. All the time, I was staying my distance from everybody wearing my mask when I was not eating alone in the kitchen. The food was delicious as usual. It is almost impossible not to eat my mother's cooking while visiting home spending precious time making memories with my family. It feels fulfilling and lures me to eat well.

When it was time to decide where to sleep, I asked my mother which bedroom she would sleep in tonight. I laughingly told her I would not sleep in the bed where she slept with a temperature of 104. She stated I should sleep in the back bedroom, jokingly reminding me that I had brought my own pillow and bed coverings as usual. I did as I was told by my mother, laughing with her about my habit of bringing my own sleep coverings.

I had a good night's sleep while lying in between my warm blanket with my head on my silk pillow slip I love dearly. The next morning, I awaken before my mother. I went to the kitchen to prepare breakfast for her. She was awakened by my stirring around in her kitchen. She stated I should go for my usual morning walk. She stated she wanted to cook breakfast. I asked if she was sure about cooking because I wanted to prepare breakfast to give her a break from cooking since she did it almost daily. My mother has a heart of gold, loves to cook, spreading love by feeding us her delicious meals.

Two weeks prior to my visit, one of our close friends and her family were diagnosed with COVID-19. My mother prepared daily meals for the family because they were sick and unable to cook for themselves. She exemplifies what it means to be a true servant to God's people. She shares her love of cooking foods to nourish them back to health.

I went for my morning walk going through downtown Eufaula, Alabama, while reminiscing on sweet memories of my childhood growing up in my small town. I love the lake that surrounds the city. I spent many of my childhood days fishing on the banks at one of the city parks. As teenagers, we fished for fun. In the summer, there were fishing rodeos with many fun times on Lake Eufaula. We watched big barges travel from Eufaula to the Georgetown, Georgia side of the lake. It was fun seeing the big boats travel through our town. These were the sweetest memories. I am overtaken by my childhood memories every time I spend the night in Eufaula when I go for morning walks.

I returned to my mother's house after my walk, feeling refreshed. As I stretched my muscles outside in front of the house, the aroma of my favorite salmon croquettes came from inside the house. By now, my taste buds are being tantalized. I imagined what it will taste like once I take the first bite of the homemade biscuits, preserved pears and salmon croquettes. I imagined what it will do for my palate as I smiled from ear to ear.

I enter the kitchen to my mother saying, "the food is ready, come on and eat." As usual, I washed my hands, fixed my plate, sat at the table, said a quick prayer, and began to throw down on this delicious southern breakfast. One of the things I like to do for family members who live out of town is to take a photo of this favorite southern breakfast and put it on Facebook for them to see. I usually brag about how my mom is spoiling me by cooking my favorite breakfast. It is a family joke now. I will say laughingly, "I was eating that good food. I did not know I was sitting there eating COVID-19." Everyone, especially my mother, will laugh. One family member who lives out of town stated, "I am so glad I missed that meal." However, before she knew we were getting infected with COVID-19, she told me how wrong it was for me to taunt them that way.

As if breakfast was not enough to fill me with COVID-19, my mother fixed lunch for us after we returned from taking care of a family matter which brought me to Eufaula in the first place. My mother wanted to show her appreciation by feeding us lunch before we all left, returning to our places of abode. Well, as might be expected, I ate home-cooked vegetables with cornbread, not knowing this was my second helping of COVID-19. Hindsight really is 20/20.

I traveled back home in a pleasant mood, knowing I could take care of the family business requiring an overnight stay. When I left, my mother was in a great mood. My trip back to Montgomery was uneventful. It was an easy and peaceful day. I am no longer working. I spend my days enjoying not having to deal with the hustle and bustle of life.

The world is in the thick of an unprecedented global health crisis with the COVID-19 pandemic. People are dying in record numbers in our country from the virus. The news is shocking. Most days, I do not turn on my television. I will read the current events on a news app on my cell phone to stay abreast of what is happening in the world to learn new updates about the virus. As if the pandemic was not enough of a crisis, our country is divisive, leading to monumental racial injustices and police brutality. It feels like every other day, week or so, another unarmed African American is being killed by the police. This country is in an uproar. It does not feel like a safe place for African Americans. These atrocities make me feel traumatized every time I hear about it.

I was recently stopped by the police. My heart started beating faster. I immediately called a family member on my car phone, so they could hear the conversation between the officer and me. I remember thinking, Lord, will I make it back home safely. When the officer exited the police car, I noticed through my rearview mirror, the officer was a black female. I begin to feel some sense of relief. However, the officer noticed my anxiety. I immediately asked what I had done to get stopped. She explained I had made an illegal turn. She explained to me why the turn was illegal. I had taken this shortcut many days, rushing to get to work to clock in before I was considered late.

My nerves were wrecked by the time I arrived in the parking lot at work that day. I called the clinical director to inform I would be in 30 minutes later for work. I had to calm my nerves before going into the building, facing my patients. I needed to regain my composure before I could perform my job duty of facilitating group therapy sessions.

Now it is Tuesday, August 25, 2020, two days after my visit home to Eufaula. My mother goes to her ophthalmologist for an eye exam, returns home feeling restless, tired, and slept most of the evening. My sister, who is currently staying with my mother to assist in caregiving, called to inform me that my mother was not feeling well. She was thinking about taking her back to the emergency room because it was unusual for her to be sleeping this long. I suggested she allow my mother to continue sleeping until the morning unless she awakens during the night. Then we will decide if she should go back to the emergency department.

My sister calls me the next morning, stating my mother was sick again. She was taken to the local emergency department for treatment. The hospital decides my mother needs inpatient care. This time a COVID-19 test was completed. My mother was placed in a private room. She was being treated for the symptoms of COVID- 19. I also was informed my Aunt, my mother's sister, was placed in the local hospital for treatment as well the same day. My mother had pneumonia in one of her lungs. My Aunt had pneumonia in both lungs.

I began to feel afraid for my mother and Aunt because I had heard the news of how severe COVID-19 could be on the elderly, especially people with an illness that compromises their immune system. I began praying to my God to cover, protect and heal my mother and my Aunt.

On Wednesday, August 26, 2020, three days later, after my trip to Eufaula with my family, I went to my ophthalmologist for my annual eye examination. They dilated my pupils and put a bright light in my eyes to check for any abnormalities. I felt fine while they were completing my yearly follow-up eye exam. No problems or changes were noted other than the prescription for my new eyeglasses.

Upon returning home from my eye exam, I started feeling restless. As the evening progressed, my head started hurting. It began to feel like the top of my head was blowing off. I was home alone. I called a family member to inform them how I was feeling. I begin to think about my mother's eye exam the day before and how she started feeling sick afterward. I started wondering if these symptoms were coincidental or more than what could be seen by the natural eyes. I wrestled with my headache all night, called my older son the next morning, explaining to him what was going on with my mother and me. I shared my concerns about COVID-19. I was not the only family member who was experiencing symptoms of COVID-19 at the time.

Before knowing for sure my mother had tested positive for COVID 19, I decided I needed to get tested. I wanted to know if I had been infected with it. I called my primary physician's office to set up an appointment to get tested. I was informed he would be out of town until the next week. I then went to the local COVID-19 Clinic, set up an appointment, and got tested. I was informed the results would be available in 3 to 5 days.

The next day after my test, I was informed my mother had tested positive for COVID-19. She was transferred to the COVID-19 Unit in the hospital. Two family members, my sister and my nephew, who were living with my mother, tested positive for the virus the same day. We all had the same symptoms of headaches, fatigue, nausea and little strength to move around. Even though I was waiting for my results, I knew I would test positive for the virus as well as several other family members. I began treating my symptoms. I quarantined myself in my home. The severity of my COVID-19 infection experience began.

"God is our refuge and strength, a very present help in trouble. Therefore, we will not fear, though the earth be removed, and the mountains be carried into the midst of the sea," Psalm 45: 1-2

The beginning of my journey, realizing I was infected with COVID-

19, was scary and uncertain initially. I had heard such negative news about this virus. I was afraid it would kill me and some of my family members who had high blood pressure, especially the older ones who had more severe health conditions. I was afraid for my mother and my aunt especially. As a Christian, I began to pray for God's deliverance and healing. I wrote a post on my Facebook page soliciting all prayer warriors to pray for my family because ten members of my immediate family had been exposed to and infected by the virus.

I was home alone. I began to wonder how I was going to survive this ordeal. Due to the virus being contagious and airborne, I alerted both of my sons. I pleaded with them not to come inside my house because I did not want them exposed or infected.

I decided I would stay in my living room, sleep on the couch near the front door just in case I needed to call the paramedics if an emergency such as difficulty breathing, shortness of breath, having a heart attack, organs shutting down happened to me. I did not know what to expect due to all the misinformation from news reported on television. After all, this was a new disease. No one knew how the virus would impact a person's immune system specifically. There was a list of symptoms reportedly found common in those already infected with the virus. Death was one. It would reportedly affect people differently. I did not know what to expect or how it would impact my immune system. I was unsure if I would have difficulty breathing or experience respiratory problems. I was so afraid for my family members and me.

I spent the first seven days on my living room couch before I regained my strength and was able to sleep in my own bed in my bedroom.

The first night, I experienced nausea, lightheaded, and could barely get up to use the bathroom. I began to have a fever and chills in the middle of the night. I continued taking medications to treat my symptoms. I started praying to God, telling Him I wanted to live to fulfill my vision of opening a Children's Culture Center, write bestselling books and be with my family again. I started thinking about God's goodness and how blessed my life was before this virus infected us. I was retired. I had not worked my job as a mental health therapist in over three months. I was living an easy, carefree life. I did not want to die from COVID-19.

I began tapping into my faith. I began believing my family members and I were going to make it through this ordeal. I stopped thinking about how many minorities had been killed by the virus. I stopped thinking about how our government had allowed this virus to spread throughout the country without any real plan of controlling it. The pandemic had already made me feel like the world was in turmoil. There was not a feeling of normalcy to what we had been accustomed to. My prayer life began to expand and explode.

I felt very weak. It felt like all my strength was gone. When I needed to move to the bathroom or get medications from the kitchen, I began calling on God to help me. I would say, "Lord, I can't move. I need your strength right now to help me get up from this couch. Lord, I feel so weak. I am your daughter. I need you, Father. Help me, Lord." The first night was very scary. I leaned on my faith to carry me through the night. I repeatedly told myself we were all going to be alright. I prayed hard, asking God not to leave or forsake my family and me. I knew I needed to change my thoughts because of feelings of despair. I made a shift in my thinking to focus on positive instead of negative things. I believed all of us would recover from this virus.

I began to think back on how I may have gotten infected since I wore a mask, stayed my six feet distance from family members and washed my hands consistently while visiting my family in Eufaula. I realized I was infected through my eyes. Three family members living in my mom's home were infected. The virus was airborne. It was in the air inside the home. I thought to myself, " I had not only eaten the virus but was breathing it in as well."

The eye exam and the light pointed in my eyes during the exam caused the virus to erupt through my eyes, entering other parts of my body. I had read the virus could cause severe problems to all organs in the body. I started praying to God, asking Him to protect my eyes, brain, heart, lungs, kidneys, liver, skin, and other parts of my body. I was specific with God when I prayed to him. I also prayed for Him to do the same for every member of my family infected by the virus.

The next day I sent out a prayer request to my Church asking my Church family to pray for me and my family members infected by the virus. As a Christian woman, I live by the scripture found in James 5:16, "The effectual fervent prayer of the righteous availeth much."

We lived in four different houses. All family members in each household were quarantined. Our family was already close-knit. We became much closer by communicating daily during this time. Each day those infected who were not hospitalized called in the morning and in the evening checking on each other.

Other relatives who live in different places across the country called to check on us. Many were scared and worried about us. They voiced their concerns, prayers and support. All of us were concerned about my mother and aunt. My mother had the best doctor who was compassionate and kind to her. He spoke directly to my niece, who lived in Maryland daily because the rest of our immediate family members were sick with the virus. He was initially concerned about my mother because of her health issues, age, and pneumonia in one of her lungs.

He moved her to the COVID Unit after her test came back positive. A day later, she began having problems with her oxygen, blood pressure, and glucose levels. She was placed on the Intensive Care Unit for closer observation and monitoring for several days. I knew my mom was a fighter. I was no longer worried or scared that she would not make it. I spoke to her daily on the phone. Like a good mother, she was concerned about me and my health. Every day her voice sounded stronger. She complained a lot about the food at the hospital being cold. Everyone knows hot food is needed to help battle the virus.

By now, I have been so sick for about three days getting up from my couch to take medications, eat a saltine cracker or a spoonful of soup because I needed food for energy to help strengthen my system. On the second day of being sick, I lost my sense of smell and taste. I could not really eat or hold food down. My stomach was nauseated, upset, and I had diarrhea. My stools were very dark in color. I knew the virus was in my stomach by now. I continued drinking hot lemon tea and juice from oranges. When I had enough strength to do it, I would stand over the steam from boiled orange peelings and sea salt for several minutes. I would also drink tea made of ginger root, lemon, honey and peppermint.

Other symptoms I experienced were fever and chills. I would awaken feeling sweaty and would easily get chills. It was a struggle to stay comfortable.

The first four to five days were the worst during my experience. Friends and family would encourage me to walk as much as possible. Walking was difficult because of the weakness, fatigue and nausea. When I awaken in the mornings, my stomach felt like it was boiling as if a war was going on inside of it. At times I would feel like I could get up from the couch to walk around in the house. Then instantaneously, the nausea would catch me off guard. Laying down for hours would be the only remedy to cure it. The nausea lasted for about seven days. One of the main symptoms of COVID-19 is it takes away all your energy, leaving you feeling weak, fatigued and tired. Sleep was an essential remedy to help me deal with COVID- 19. My usual sleep pattern was interrupted and off schedule.

During this illness, the turning point was my prayer life and my faith that God would heal us. On the third day, when my mom went to the Intensive Care Unit. I had to go up a notch or level with my prayers to God. The scripture Psalm 27 says, "The Lord is my light and my salvation, whom shall I fear. Though an army besiege me, my heart will not fear. Though war break out against me, even then will I be confident."

I realized this virus is spiritual warfare. It attacks our bodies but also attacks our spirit. I know the God I serve is bigger than COVID-19. I had to speak to this virus through my spirit. I began to claim victory and healing in my spirit. I declared COVID-19 would not take me or any of my family member's life.

I talked to God every day while I was lying down or walking through my house. I know there were times I could not carry myself to the bathroom or to the kitchen to get my medications. It was during those times God carried me.

I spoke to my Heavenly Father God as if he was my earthly father. My conversation with God would be something like this. "God, this is your daughter Mary Ann. Lord, I need you to help me go to the kitchen. Lord, I need you to help me to go to the bathroom. Lord, I am weak, but I know you are strong. Please help me, Jesus. I need you right now. Lord, I cannot make it without you. Lord, there is nobody here except you and me. I need you right now."

Your word says in Deuteronomy 31:6 says, "Be strong and of good courage, do not fear nor be afraid of them; for the Lord your God, He is the one who goes with you. He will not leave or forsake you." Whenever I prayed or talked directly to God, He came through for me. I had to speak to this giant of COVID-19 in my life.

One day while speaking on the phone with my mom while she was in the Intensive Care Unit, I was trying to uplift and encourage her. I said, "Mama, we are just going through a little storm right now." My mama said to me, "This ain't no storm, it's just a little wind." I said, "Glory, mama, if you see what you are going through as a little wind, then I am going through just a little sprinkle of rain." I began to praise God for her strength and faith in God. My mama was in the hospital with pneumonia in one of her lungs, on an oxygen machine having a near-death experience, yet she saw herself going through "Just a little wind." I knew we were going to recover from this virus.

The days of COVID-19 were not always this easy. There were days when my mom would talk about getting her will in order. She discussed what she wanted to leave for her grandchildren. Those were the days I prayed harder. I had to really stretch my faith. I know death is a part of living, but I did not want to discuss death and dying while we were battling COVID-19. My mind frame was positive and optimistic. I kept praying for my family and me to be healed.

I have not mentioned much about my aunt, who was positive for COVID-19, had pneumonia in both lungs. Her situation was bleaker than the rest of us. After being in the hospital in Eufaula for two days, her children from Georgia came to take her back to a hospital in Georgia. She began to start eating, talking and improving. She stayed in the hospital there for several days and was released to rehabilitation for 21 days. The reports we received from her children, grandchildren were positive and encouraging.

Be careful for nothing; but in everything by prayer and supplication with thanksgiving let your requests be made know to God.

Philippians 4:6-7

Chapter 2
Surviving While Infected with COVID-19

H aving COVID 19 can be terrifying because, by now, everyone in the United States knows at least one or two people who have died from it. As I am writing today, over 250,000 thousand Americans have died from this virus. I believe being healthy physically, mentally and spiritually is a good regimen to help you survive while being infected with the virus. Prior to being infected with the virus, I had a routine of exercising at least 30 or more minutes, taking multiple vitamins to include Vitamin C and D3, every day. I now take Elderberry with antioxidants to help support my immune system. It is important to have a healthy immune system to fight COVID-19, as it attacks the immune system.

God and I unknowingly were preparing my body for the fight against the virus days before becoming infected. I had changed my diet, exercised daily and was taking vitamins to boost my immune system. I went on a very strict diet plan where I participated in a 21 days healthy food challenge eating only stir-fried meats, vegetables, all healthy foods with no white rice, bread, potatoes, starchy carbohydrates and sugars. I had visited my primary physician two weeks prior to my family visit. I was informed I no longer had diabetes because I had lost weight due to my lifestyle changes. I was feeling positive about my changes. I had a positive mental outlook. My mental health was challenged due to the recent police killings of African Americans throughout the country, my fear of being exposed to and infected with the virus. My spirituality was strong and solid. God had me working on a prevention plan; I did not know I would need to fight COVID-19.

It has been difficult having to deal with life changes due to this pandemic. My church started having live-streamed worship services. I continued worshipping with my church family during live-streamed services every Sunday. My faith and my prayer life were stronger. I continued praising God amidst the pandemic. I continually remember the twenty-third Psalm when I am dealing with a crisis such as COVID- 19, and all we have going on today.

It says, "The Lord is my shepherd, I shall not want. He maketh me to lie down in green pastures; He leads me beside the still waters. He restores my soul; He leads me in the paths of righteousness for His name's sake. Yea, though I walk through the valley of the shadow of death, I will fear no evil. For you are with me; Your rod and your staff, they comfort me. You prepare a table before me in the presence of my enemies; You anoint my head with oil; My cup runs over. Surely goodness and mercy shall follow me; All the days of my life; And I will dwell in the house of the Lord forever." I am a strong believer that goodness and mercy shall follow my family and me.

By day # 5 of being infected, I had a come to Jesus meeting with COVID-19. I literally had to introduce COVID-19 to my God. The conversation went something like this, "Now, COVID-19, you may have power, but you do not have as much power as my God. You cannot have me. You cannot have my family. You may be lingering in our body, but we are winning. Our God is more powerful than COVID-19. COVID-19, meet my God." I spoke to the giant of COVID-19. I believed every word I spoke as I was speaking it. As a Christian woman, I have been taught to speak to your giants. God is more powerful than any of the giants we are facing. He gave me the strength to speak to COVID-19 even when I was feeling weak, I felt strong in the Lord.

By day #7, I could get up, walk around more in my house and fix food to eat. I fixed a big pot of homemade vegetable soup and made a pan of cornbread. My sense of taste and smell had not returned. I was still experiencing nausea and fatigue. My energy level was low, but I was happy to be able to stand for at least one hour without having to lay back down. I could not really taste the soup or cornbread I cooked, but I ate it anyway because I knew I needed food to restore my strength. I continued taking vitamins, drinking hot teas, coffee and everything hot hoping to get rid of the virus.

Also, on day #7, I took a bath, washed my hair and started sleeping in my bed in my bedroom. I felt better getting a restful night of sleep.

Even when I did not feel like it, I started eating breakfast, lunch and dinner, which was maybe one or two spoons of the vegetable soup juice with cornbread mashed up in it. I looked at myself in the mirror, noticing my face looked frail and not as full as normal. I thought I looked older than usual. I realized I had lost weight because I was able to eat only small portions of food during the early days of being sick. I also started washing my bed covers every morning, thinking it would facilitate a quicker recovery. All other family members were getting stronger and better, as well. We continued talking to my mother daily and to each other.

"We are inevitably our brother's keeper because we are our brother's brother. Whatever affects one directly affects all indirectly."

Martin Luther King, Jr.

Chapter 3
A Strong Support System with COVID-19

A strong support network is essential in recovering from COVID- 19. My God was my strongest supporter. I believed He would never leave or forsake me, as stated in Hebrews 13:5. God was with me throughout those days. I was unable to move, although I was sick from COVID-19. I know I never would have made it without God and my strong support system.

My close friends and my family made a big difference in my healing process. Family members and friends called daily, provided food, water, nutritional liquids to drink, medicine or whatever I asked them to bring. They would drop it off in front of the door for me to get it. Many of them waited in their car, called me to make sure I could walk outside to get the food or whatever they dropped off for me.

I have a ton of Facebook friends who messaged to check on me. Others texted with an encouraging word, scriptures and sent get well messages.

When I started to regain some of my strength, I joined a PUSH (Pray Until Something Happens) prayer line, where friends and Church of Christ members had already been praying for my family and me. I felt encouraged to know my Church, as well as other brethren in the Church of Christ, had been praying for my family and me to recover from the virus.

One Sunday, I asked one of my best friends to bring me soup, salad and breadsticks from Olive Garden, she delivered on time. Another day a best friend brought a Popeyes fried chicken sandwich with French fries. I was unable to taste anything but ate as much as I could to maintain my strength. Another friend called and asked what I needed her to do for me. I told her I wanted her to cook chicken and rice soup with homemade cornbread when my taste returned. A few days later, I called and told her my taste was returning. I asked her to fix the chicken and rice soup. She fixed a huge pot of soup, cornbread and delivered it to my front door. I was able to eat that chicken soup for about four days. I remembered my mama cooking chicken and rice soup for me when I was sick as a child. It always seemed to make me feel better, just like the soup my friend brought me to eat.

As I was dealing with COVID-19, I had a strong support network cheering me to healing and recovery. My needs were being met by my sons, family members and friends. I was reminded of the scripture Matthew7:12, which says, "Therefore all things whatsoever ye would that men should do to you; Do ye even so to them: for this is the law of prophets." I consider myself to be kind and generous to others. I have a passion for helping and serving others. I always have, and I always will. It is my calling to serve, help and empower others just as I have throughout my almost four decades of working in my profession as a social work practitioner.

When I felt at my lowest point during the onset of this virus, the main focus was to get well and feel better. I did not know who or what I would need other than medicine. I praise God today; my and my family's needs were met. My oldest son was my rock. I depended on him to provide the things I needed daily. He came through for me. The Bible says in Proverbs 22:6, "Train up a child in the way he should go and when he is old, he will not depart." I thank God for allowing me to train my son. I am even more thankful he did not depart from me when I was sick. He had an overnight trip planned to Atlanta and asked if I would be ok. I told him to go since it was already planned. During that night, I felt so sick at one of my lowest point during this experience. I wondered whom I should call upon to get medications for the congestion I was experiencing. My youngest son had been infected with COVID -19 as well. He was quarantined in Tuskegee, Al. My Nigerian family friends came through for me, bringing the medications for the congestion. They also brought a special medication from Nigeria used to combat COVID-19. I took the medications resting well that night.

I believe doing good pays off. I believe if you do good, good will follow you. Philippians 4:19 says, "But my God shall supply all your need according to his riches in glory by Christ Jesus." My support system provided all of my needs during my COVID- 19 crisis.

I was filled with God's word daily. One of my daily morning tasks is to read a daily devotional, text it to my sons and share it with my Facebook friends on messenger. I continued reading my devotional on the days I was able to get up from the couch. I continued sending encouraging words to my sons and Facebook friends on messenger. I needed to maintain my spiritual growth, grounding to keep a sense of normalcy while battling COVID -19. I had spoken that my God was more powerful than COVID -19. I had to put actions to my words. Faith without works is dead. I have a working and sustaining faith. I needed to keep my spiritual needs feed by reading and speaking God's word to my giant of COVID -19.

It is important to have a close relationship with God and a strong prayer life daily to make it in our world today. It was necessary to be close to God and strengthen my prayer life daily. Having a strong faith is extremely important. My faith was tried, tested and stretched during this COVID-19 experience. Faith is an action word. I had to put some words and work behind my faith to survive COVID-19.

James 2:17-18 says, "Even so faith, if it hath not works, is dead, being alone. Yea, a man may say, Thou hast faith, and I have works. Shew me thy faith without thy works and I will shew thee my faith by my works."

Chapter 4
Recovering while infected with COVID- 19

R ecovery is an ongoing process. I am finding there are residual effects of COVID-19.

On Day # 10, I began to regain more strength. My sense of taste and smell began to return. I was able to taste food better. My stools began to look normal again. I was able to walk more inside the house. I felt like taking baths daily and getting dressed. I was beginning to feel somewhat like my normal self again. My voice was getting stronger. I began to praise God more for our healing. I had completed my first round of antibiotics. I believed I was healing and recovering from the virus. Other family members were feeling stronger and better, as well.

On Day #12, I noticed a skin rash on my inner arms. It began to spread on my legs and thighs as days passed. I researched the symptoms of

COVID-19. Skin rash showed up as a symptom. It did not itch. It was just present. None of my family members who were infected with COVID-19 noticed a rash.

On Day # 14, on a Friday, I went back to my primary care physician to get a retest to see if the virus was still present in my body. My doctor looked at the rash on my arms and was puzzled. He stated he had seen over one hundred patients, and I was the first to have a skin rash. He made a referral for me to see a dermatologist. He jokingly said, "Mary Ann, you are weird." My response to him was, "I don't mind being weird. I just don't want to be sick."

It took three days for the results to return. On Day #17, Monday, I received a call from my doctor's office informing me my COVID -19 test results were positive again. I was placed on another round of antibiotics. I was also informed to remain in quarantine for 10 more days.

Two of my family members tested negative for COVID-19 on Day #14.

On Day #15, my mother was released from the hospital. She was discharged home with oxygen tubes and an oxygen tank due to changes in her oxygen levels. Her doctor wanted her to go to rehabilitation for 21 days before returning home. She told him she would go home with homemaker services receiving rehab therapy at home.

I was able to face time with my mom when she got home. I was so happy to see her and to know she was recovering well. She was talking stronger. Her body looked frail. I knew she had to fight hard to continue healing from COVID-19. I felt uneasy seeing the oxygen tubes in her nose, but none the less I felt happy she was well enough to return home.

After talking with and face timing with my mama, I began to praise God for bringing her back home, keeping, covering, protecting and healing her. I began singing the song, "This Aint No Ordinary Praise and This Aint No Ordinary Worship." God had worked miracles in our lives.

After all these days of fighting COVID-19, we did not lose one family member. All 10 of us are still here. We are all alive. I give God the highest praise as he continues to keep us.

One of my favorite scriptures is Philippians 4:13. "I can do all things through Christ who strengthens me" Not only did I pray my way through, I praised my way through as we were recovering. I know with God all things are possible. God specializes in impossibilities. He comes through for his children in miraculous ways. He did it for my family and me.

I cried out to God, and He heard my cry. Psalm 61:2 says. "From the end of the earth I call to You when my heart is faint: lead me to the rock that is higher than I." God is my rock, my healer and my deliverer. He continues to bless my family and me on this road to recovery from COVID-19. Hallelujah! Glory be to all mighty God.

Upon receiving the news of a positive COVID Test, I began to praise God for my life, health, and total healing. Psalm 104: 33 says, "I will sing to the Lord all my life. I will sing praise to my God as long as I live." I focused on the goodness of God and how far he has brought me from my couch to sleeping in my bed, getting back to eating healthy, exercising and taking care of my own personal needs.

I had not fully recovered from my COVID-19 ordeal. I continued to maintain an optimistic outlook. I thought of the goodness of God. Even though the virus was still lingering in my body, I felt healthy. I had fully returned to my daily routine. I nurtured my mind, body and soul, thinking I would soon recover from COVID-19 once the body rash cleared up.

On Day # 30, I went back to my primary physician to get a third COVID-19 test. I was instructed to remain quarantined until I receive my results the following Monday. I will continue to fight the good fight of faith, waiting until my change comes. Until I receive the test results, I claimed healing and victory from COVID-19. The rash is still present on my arms, legs and thighs. My sense of taste and smell has not fully returned. I was able to taste some foods and slightly smell strong odors. My voice was stronger. I was able to complete chores around the house. I was able to start my exercise regimen at home.

After receiving the news about my third COVID-19 test being positive after 33 days of dealing with this virus, my mood was a little gloomy. In my mind, I was thinking the rash had something to do with the positive results. I felt one hundred percent back to my normal self. I was able to complete my daily routine at home. My family members tried to comfort me by saying the tests were inaccurate, and I should not worry.

Again, my faith was being tested. I had to have another conversation with COVID-19 and my God. It went something like this, "OK God, I know You got me covered. I know this is another test of my faith to see if I will allow the devil to intercede in my thoughts; still, my joy causes me to get depressed and not trust you, God. But Lord, I know there is a purpose for this test. There is a lesson for me to learn from this experience. COVID 19, my God is bigger and has more power than you can ever imagine. I will learn my lesson and use this test as my testimony."

God allowed me to quickly change my sullen mood into one of being grateful. I started looking at how much I have recovered from being sick, nauseated, fatigued, unable to smell or taste anything. I began to count my many blessings. I had a praise party by myself with an attitude of gratitude. I knew I had to stay away from people, wear a mask, and keep my distance of six feet or more if someone came to my house for some reason. I knew God had a greater purpose for this experience. He chose me because I was strong enough for the test. I also knew Satan leveled up in his attempts to derail my faith in God. He tried, but it did not work.

I knew I needed to come up with a strategy and recovery plan. I started using the same skills I taught my patients to use while recovering from a mental illness. I began to change my negative thoughts by replacing them with positive thoughts. I know every negative feeling begins when negative thoughts are present. I rebuked those negative thoughts. I began looking at the many blessings I am experiencing in this season of my life. I started looking for the good things in my life. I know we usually get what we expect in our lives. I know bad things happen to good people. It is not so much of what happens to us but our perception about what is happening to us. I began to read inspirational messages. I began using mindfulness skills, experiencing each moment as a blessing from God. I prayed, talking to God throughout my day and asking for His guidance. I listened to meditational music to calm down and relax. I cannot say enough about being grateful and having an attitude of gratitude. Each morning I wrote down at least five things on my gratitude list. I began my exercise regimen to boost my happy hormones. I also talked to family and friends for support daily. I watched a little television. I read the information on my cell phone news app to stay updated on current events and the coronavirus.

It has been over thirty days of recovery for me and my family members being infected with COVID-19. Most of us have returned to our pre-COVID-19 exposure days of what we described as normal living during this pandemic. I decided I will return to get retested once the rash cleared up on my legs and arms.

It has been over fourteen days since my last positive test results. I can say being infected with the virus has been a life-changing experience for my family and me. Personally, I am being transformed in a positive way with a closer daily walk with God. I feel closer to Him. My spiritual foundation has been exemplified. I know my God in a more personal way. I know He has got me covered. God keeps me strong. He is a miracle-working God. His miracles are manifested daily in my life.

Recovery has been difficult for one of my family members, who relapsed back to using ineffective ways to cope with the COVID-19 experience. This pandemic has created a major giant for many to deal with because of being quarantined, isolating us from family and friends. Others are terrified of getting the virus. I was one of them before I was infected. I followed the CDC guidelines daily. It still happened to nine of my family members and me.

I will continue being positive about my experience because I have learned to look at the blessings in this lesson during this season of my life. I learned to celebrate each breath I breathe, embracing each day as if it is my last day. I learned I should take nothing for granted.

Life can change in a matter of minutes. Nothing will be the same. I learned to appreciate the time spent with my family and friends because we never know when we may lose one. I am still recovering. I believe this virus will be around for longer than what has been indicated by the scientist. It will continue to impact our physical, mental and spiritual health. I will continue my walk with God because I know He is bigger and more powerful than COVID-19.

God worked a miracle in my family because not one of us died due to being infected by the virus. We are all stronger in many aspects of our lives, especially spiritually. While being sick with the virus, I knew I needed coping strategies to sustain my physical and mental health.

Chapter 5
Coping Strategies to Manage Stress and Anxiety While Sick with COVID-19

A s I was experiencing COVID-!9, I thought of some coping strategies I taught to my clients and patients during my years of empowering them to manage crisis situations. I have listed the strategies I used below as a tool guide for managing while dealing with the crisis of COVID-19.

1. Accept Your Illness for what it is and get immediate medical treatment

The first step to solving a problem is to acknowledge the problem exists. Once you realize you are experiencing COVID-19 symptoms, schedule an appointment to get tested for the virus. Sometimes it is difficult to acknowledge we have an illness, especially the novel coronavirus. Many times, we are in denial, attempting to hide what we are experiencing. Sometimes we are afraid to admit we have a problem. The misinformation and the fears reported about the virus initially by the media were scary, bringing uncertainty feelings. It contributed to how people responded. I was afraid to tell anyone outside of my immediate at first until I realized I needed prayer warriors to pray for my family. At first, I was afraid to get it. Then, I felt embarrassed to say I was sick with COVID-19.

I realized I should not allow fear to manifest itself in my mind while I was sick with the virus. I made a choice to choose my faith over my fear. Choosing faith increased my level of optimism. I have taught my patients to maintain a positive outlook while going through a crisis. Studies have shown people who maintain an optimistic attitude and repeat positive affirmations will recover faster than patients who maintain a negative outlook. Studies have shown the length of stay in a hospital for an optimistic patient is shorter than those who are pessimistic.

2. Follow Doctor's Advice and Take Medications as prescribed

It is important to get tested when experiencing symptoms or realize you have been exposed to the virus. It is reported some people are asymptomatic of the virus. They experience no symptoms even though they are infected with the virus. This is one reason the virus is so dangerous. It can be a death sentence for aging and sick relatives. A young person who is asymptomatic has been exposed to or infected with the virus, experiencing no symptoms can transmit it to an elderly family member unknowingly. It has been reported that 8 in 10 people who have died from COVID-19 were age 65 or older.

I was extremely concerned about the possibility of my mother and aunt dying from the virus because of their age and current medical conditions.

It is extremely important for anyone who thinks they have been exposed to or experiencing symptoms to get a COVID-19 test immediately.

One of my fears was I would expose and infect others to the virus. I did not want anyone to get sick because of me. I have in the past and will continue in the present to follow the CDC's prevention guidelines.

Take your medications as prescribed by your doctor.

Follow all other instructions given for your medical regimen while sick with COVID-19

3. Focus on Faith and Spirituality

As a woman of faith, I have been taught I should keep the faith when I am confronted with adversities, trials, hard times and when life is not going as planned. I was taught fear means false expectations appearing real. Often when we fear something, we are expecting the worst outcome. A Christian is supposed to be strong and depend on God to bring them out of their hard times by tapping into their spirituality. We are taught to expect the best, not the worst.

After I was diagnosed with COVID-19, I realized I would not make it through this ordeal without tapping into my faith and spiritual beliefs. I reminded myself about my walk with God. I thought of how he had delivered me from sickness and adversities in the past. I know from experience trials, sickness and hard times come to test our faith in God. Real faith is tested and tried. My COVID-19 experience definitely tested and tried my faith. My faith was stretched.

This experience increased my faith. It showed me believing in and trusting God was my saving grace. I could not see my way through with my natural eyes. My spiritual eyes reassured me I was going to heal from COVID-19. I knew this battle was not mine to fight physically. It was a spiritual battle; only my faith could conquer. I am still winning with God. I am still focusing on my faith and my spirituality. Each day, I decided to tap into my spiritual walk with God, hoping to expect good things to happen.

Always focus on your faith and spirituality when dealing with any giant in your life. Faith gives us hope for better things to come.

Hebrews 11:I states, "Now faith is the substance of things hoped for, the evidence of things not seen." Expect good things to come. Always believe you will get better and heal from COVID-19.

4. Solicit prayers from all Christians, family and friends

A strong prayer life is essential to a Christian's daily walk with God. It keeps us connected to God. It is my way of communicating my needs to God. It is important to pray for yourself daily. As I was going through my COVID-19 experience, I realized I needed prayers from others. I know the effectual fervent prayers of the righteous avails much. I solicited prayers from family, friends and fellow Christian. I knew somebody's prayers would reach the ears of God. I figured the more prayers were sent up to God for my family and me, the better.

Knowing prayer warriors were lifting my family up to God made me feel like I was not alone when I was sick. It is empowering to know others care enough to pray for you. It also gives you the strength to make it through the test. It helps push you forward to the other side of the illness. It gives you something to look forward to. It feels good to share your trials and test with others, so when you do your victory dance, others can dance with you because their prayers for you were answered. It also allowed me to turn my test into a testimony of how God answered my prayers. Praying motivated me to continue praising my way through this giant of COVID-19.

5. Get on a prayer line with Christian Brothers and Sisters as soon as you can.

Once I started regaining my strength to get up off my couch, I was able to dial into a prayer line called PUSH (Pray until something happens). Of course, when we pray, we are expecting good and not bad results. It is good to know when people are praying on your behalf. However, when you hear the voice of a prayer warrior talking to God on your behalf, the impact is much more powerful. Hearing your name being called out to God is like hearing your name called out at the Academy award. It is exhilarating.

Choose a prayer line to solicit God's healing on your behalf. The saying goes, "There is strength in numbers." I like to think about it this way. If, for some reason, my voice does not reach the ears of God, one of my prayer warrior's voices will.

6. Maintain contact with Support System to include family, friends, medical team and prayer warriors

This pandemic has caused many people to stay at home alone, fearing they will be exposed or infected by the virus. We are social human beings. We need contact with and support of others to help us survive this unprecedented global health crisis. I prefer seeing my family and friends face to face. This pandemic changed that. Now we communicate more using social media and talking on the cell phone. We need each other. We need support from each other, especially when we are sick or experiencing a crisis.

First, always stay connected to God or your higher power source. Speak to your higher power source daily. I called upon and spoke with my God daily many times throughout my sickness.

Also, maintain daily contact with your support system of family, friends, fellow Christians, prayer warriors and your medical team for support. Even God gave Adam a support person in Eve when He made her from Adam's rib. He did not want Adam to be alone. It is difficult to be alone when you are sick. Initially, it was scary for me. I had to tap into my faith and power source to realize I was alone physically, but my God was with me spiritually all the way. A strong support system is a must for managing and sustaining your health during a crisis. You will heal sooner knowing you have the support of family and friends.

7. Pray for self.

It is great when our family, friends, Christian brothers and sisters pray for us. It is a must for us to pray for ourselves. It seems strange if I want others to pray for me, and I do not pray for myself. I must maintain my connection to my God, my power source. I know my needs more so than anyone else. My family and friends have their own burdens to bear. I trust them to talk to God on my behalf. Life happens, and they may be so tied up with a crisis of their own. They may forget to pray on my behalf due to their own unforeseen circumstance. I pray for myself daily without ceasing. I prayed continuously throughout my days, asking God for healing, guidance and deliverance from COVID-19. I also pray for my strength and endurance to deal with any dilemma I face.

8. Maintain a healthy diet eating hot foods and drinking hot liquids

Good health begins with a healthy diet. Proper nutrition keeps us strong and helps to strengthen our immune system. A strong immune system can prevent or protect us from an illness. It was difficult to eat for the first few days of having COVID-19. I forced myself to eat and drink plenty of water to stay hydrated. I ate something if it was only saltine crackers with a tablespoon full of soup. Our body needs proper nutrition to give us the energy to help us fight whatever illness we are experiencing.

COVID-19 took away my strength to take care of my daily needs and fulfill my daily tasks around my house. There were days I did not have enough strength to get up off my couch. It was during those times God carried me to get food from the kitchen or use the bathroom. Food is our body's energy source. Eat as much nutritional food as you can to facilitate a speedy healing process.

It was reported eating hot foods and drinking hot liquids helped to heal and manage COVID-19. I drank at least two hot cups of lemon tea and other hot liquids daily to speed up my healing and recovery.

10. Get proper sleep

COVID-19 affected my sleep pattern. Prior to being infected, I enjoyed eight hours of sleep nightly. It was difficult to maintain my sleep regimen while sick. The virus was indifferent to my sleep patterns. The first few nights of being infected, my stomach was boiling over and making loud noises. I experienced fever and chills. I could not maintain my regular sleep regimen. There were also times when I slept a lot during the day instead of at night.

I read an article from our health experts, indicating the best remedy for a strong immune system included taking vitamins C and D, maintain a nutritional diet, getting proper sleep, and having less stress. Proper sleep reportedly is seven to nine-hour each night to help function at your best. Sleep patterns will vary for each person.

Proper sleep is important for overall health. It is especially important to get proper sleep to facilitate the healing process.

11. Exercise as soon as you are able (Walk around in house)

Medical professionals, family members and close friends encouraged me to walk around as much as possible. They stated that lying down for long periods would cause the virus to get in my lungs, making it difficult to breathe. Little did they know, the first three days, my body was so weak and fatigued I could barely move. I was thankful I was able to get up just to go to the kitchen to take my medications, eat the small amount of foods and drink the liquids I could barely swallow.

As the days passed, when I regained more energy, I was able to walk around more frequently inside my house. On day #14, I was able to walk around and exercise more.

12. Think the best and not the worst

I have been a mental health therapist for many years. Teaching the power of positive thinking as one of the keys elements to healing from a crisis or traumatic situation was my focal point during therapy sessions. Our thoughts are powerful. They can change the trajectory of our outlook on solving problems. Often when confronted with a perceived negative situation, we are more inclined to think of a negative outcome.

We become participants and controllers of our destiny when we learn the skill of stopping our negative thinking by replacing it with positive thinking. It takes awareness of what we are thinking while consistently practicing changing our thought process. Our lives can be transformed by our thoughts, just as I was transformed during my family's COVID-19 experience.

Negative thinking holds us hostage and keeps us stuck in our circumstances. It can also contribute to feeling sorry or having a victim's mentality. When facilitating group therapy sessions, I often made a comparison of a child sitting on a training pot and a client having a pity party. "When you sit on a pity pot, all you get is a ring around your rump." Negative thinking can cause negative feelings, stagnation, prevent moving forward and healing from the current circumstance.

I learned the skill of reframing one's perception about a situation is powerful for change and growth. I had to reframe my initial perception about how COVID-19 would impact my family's life. I reframed my thoughts and expectations. I believed God was going to heal us without any of us dying to COVID-19.

Do not watch television until after feeling stronger because of all the negative news and its impact on our minds. I could not bear hearing about the increased death rate of COVID-19 patients. It is important to think positively and not listen to negative reports.

15. Listen to soft mediational music

Listening to quiet, soft and meditational music helped me feel calm when I was anxious or restless during my sickness from COVID-19. At night when I was unable to sleep, I listened to meditational music sessions to feel relaxed. Music is said to calm the wildest beast. I considered COVID-19 to be a wild beast at the time. It is an unprecedented pandemic that is out of control, terrorizing and killing people throughout the world.

Listening to music can provide a brief escape from your current situation. It helps you forget the current situation, if only for a brief time frame. It is an effective coping strategy for music lovers. It helped me survive during my days and nights of being sick with COVID-19.

16. Talk to family and friends daily

Maintain communication with family and friends daily. I felt comfortable talking to my family daily to stay updated on their condition as well as to keep them abreast of mine. We could not talk face to face because of being quarantined. It helped my recovery, knowing my family members were improving day by day. I could devote most of my efforts to caring for myself. Self-preservation is my number one priority and one of my core beliefs at this stage in my life. I knew I needed to focus on my healing.

Talking to family and friends daily encouraged and uplifted me to move forward. It showed they cared for my wellbeing just as I cared for theirs.

17. Stay as close to your daily routine as possible

It is difficult to maintain a normal routine when feeling sick, especially the first few days of being infected with COVID-19. Having a daily routine is the last thing to focus on. Feeling better and being able to move around to meet your needs is what I thought about throughout my sickness with COVId-19. Attending to daily household needs was last on my mind at the beginning. Once I regained my strength, was able to walk around in my home, I thought about the importance of getting back on a daily schedule. It was difficult at first. It was after day #10 of being infected I felt strong enough to attempt to clean my house, working toward getting back to my daily routine.

18. Read a daily devotional or inspirational words every morning

Reading a daily devotional with words of inspiration has been a big part of my adult life. It allows me to meditate on God's word. It sets the stage for my day. It is a jump start for my day. I tried to continue my daily devotional readings when I was able to sit up to read it. God's words are powerful and encouraged me throughout my COVID-19 experience.

When dealing with any illness, hearing encouraging words are like a balm to a sore spot. It soothes the mind, gives hope of healing and recovering. Inspirational words and faith work together as a tag team to victory. It helped me believe I would heal from COVID-19. Reading my daily devotional and inspirational words encouraged me to keep fighting COVID-19. My family and I are still winning.

19. Write daily gratitude listing at least five things

It may be asked why anyone would think about having gratitude during this pandemic, especially someone infected by it. Gratitude is focusing on the good things in our lives. It is being thankful for what we have. It is taking a moment to appreciate the things we often take for granted, like having a home, food, clean water, family, friends and social media. There are many things to be grateful for while experiencing the sickness.

I focused on the good things in my life. While facilitating groups or counseling sessions, I consistently reminded my patients to look for the good in all situations. There is always something good, even in bad situations. I began to thank God I was able to breathe on my own. I was grateful for my home with all the basic necessities like electricity, water to drink and bathe, food in my pantry and refrigerator. I was grateful God allowed me to be alive.

COVID-19 did not kill my family members or me. I was grateful my illness did not require me to be hospitalized. I was also grateful my mom was being treated well while in the hospital while her condition was being closely monitored. I was grateful for my faith. I was grateful God chose me to withstand the test. My faith is stronger as a result of my COVID-19 experience. I was grateful for my relationship with God. I could feel His presence around me when I felt alone and afraid.

Making a daily gratitude list allows you to look at what is good in your life. It gives you the strength to push forward by focusing on what is right instead of what is wrong. When we are grateful for small things, God knows He can trust us with bigger and better things. My walk with God is closer than before my COVID-19 experience. I am grateful for healing, deliverance and protection from God. He favors me. I will sing His praises all the days of my life.

20. Practice Mindfulness when feeling better to enlighten your mood

Mindfulness is a type of meditation focusing on being intensely aware of your sensory perceptions (taste, touch, feel, hear and see) and what you feel at that moment without judgment. Often times when I am sitting outside on my patio area, I practice mindfulness by looking up into the beautiful blue sky through my green tress with just a hint of sunshine peeking through the trees with the wind blowing lightly on the leaves. I hear the birds singing. I experience the moment without judgment. I am consciously aware of my thoughts about God's wonderful creation. I am feeling calm, relaxed and in awe.

Mindfulness allows an escape from my concerns to be at peace within myself. I can experience it for an hour before I literally return to my reality. It takes practice and consistency to allow your mind to focus on the moment, not judging it. Mindfulness will allow you to experience a boost in your mood.

21. Take a hot bath or shower as soon as you feel like getting up

The first day I had enough strength to take a hot bath, I felt as though I had experienced a miracle after being ill for seven days. There were times I had a fever, chills and felt sweaty. Taking a hot bath was like magic to my body, mind and soul. I felt clean and relaxed. The water soothed my body, putting me in a calm and relaxed mood.

There is nothing like taking a long bath or shower, feeling clean and getting into a bed with fresh linen. The old saying, "I slept like a baby," was how I felt after taking a hot bath soaking in the water until it turned cold. It was the most restful night I experienced after being sick for one week. Warm fresh baths or showers will improve your mood. It facilitates feeling calm and relaxed. It gives an escape from reality. Remember the Calgon soap commercial from back in the day. It advertised how "Calgon takes me away." Soaking in a good hot bath or a hot shower will take you away by relieving stress and anxiety.

22. Talk to positive people on the telephone

Any time you are feeling down and out, sick or experiencing a crisis, talk to someone uplifting, encouraging and optimistic. Stay away from people who have a sad story when you talk to them. Sometimes, family members and close friends can be pessimistic or negative. Avoid them. COVID-9 has killed so many people. Do not listen to someone who wants to focus on the COVID-19 death rate. Sometimes people with good intentions can subtly be negative by telling you how bad you look when you are sick. I was already my own worst critic in that area. Sick people need to hear encouraging words and not negative ones.

While sick with COVID-19, I wanted to hear encouraging words from family and friends. A couple of my friends told me, "You got things to accomplish. We need you to get well." I felt hopeful by those words of encouragement. I began to pray to God, asking him to heal me so I could fulfill my unmet goals and dreams. I was looking forward to the future. I felt positive when I thought about the goals I wanted to accomplish listed on my vision board.

23. Solicit prayers from Facebook friends, prayer warriors and keep them updated as your recover

Social media has proven a viable resource during this pandemic. We can communicate with masses of people by a simple click on our laptops and cell phones. Facebook happens to be one of the popular apps where you can have thousands of people to become your friend. I usually check into my Facebook account once or twice daily to read updated posts from my family and friends.

Some people are quiet and reserved when discussing medical issues in public outlets. I have experienced the power of prayer when other people pray to God on my behalf. I have experienced positive results when posting a prayer request for my Facebook family and friends. I know God answer prayers. I believe the more Christians pray for each other, the better the results. God hears us. Also, when you know others are praying for your healing, it feels like the burden is shared. It gives a connection to others who also share your pain.

Exposing your illness of COVID-19 is like a doubled edge sword. It may release any shame one may feel when exposed or infected. It can also be a way to keep others from wanting to be around you even after being healed. Many people fear they will catch it and will run from you. I understand this fear because I felt the same way before I was infected. This virus is so new, and there remain uncertainties related to it.

24. Ask Church members to pray for you.

Being Christians allows one to have a deeper relationship and connection with other Christians. I have heard the statement that God does not hear the prayer of a sinner. Even though we are Christians, we still sin. There is no perfect person. I feel a close connection with my Church members. I consider them my Church family. Some know me very well and can attest to my faithfulness. I solicited prayers from my Church family. I know the prayers of the righteous avails much. I know God heard and answered our prayers.

Do not be afraid to ask others to pray for you. Ask your church members to pray with and for you. We are our brothers' keeper. We need to keep the prayer line open to God. He wants to hear from us. We need Him daily. I prayed continually throughout my illness to God without ceasing.

Part 11
Changes and the Impacts During Pandemic

"Change is inevitable. Growth is optional."
John C. Maxwell

Chapter 6
Changes During COVID-19 Pandemic

S ince March of this year, our lives changed as the coronavirus began to spread throughout the world. Our country shut down, trying to prevent the spread of the disease but to no avail. It was reported in the news that our government leaders knew this virus was deadly, failed to prepare a plan to combat the pandemic in our country, failed to inform the American people just how severe this virus would attack our bodies. Like many Americans and people from other countries, we were afraid to be infected because no one knew how to treat it. The CDC began to set guidelines to prevent the spread of the virus.

Our world has changed. People are communicating more and connecting on social media. Many Americans are working remotely from home using social media connections.

The African American has been devastated by the pandemic's impact with more deaths, loss of business, unemployment, lack of health care, domestic violence, and increased poverty. It was reported by the US CDC that African Americans are just twice as likely to die than white people from COVID-19.

When the pandemic began initially, my mind and body were functioning on my "emergency pilot mode." I was anxious, feeling uneasy about going outside of my home to shop or work, fearing I would be exposed to the virus. I followed the safety guidelines suggested by CDC and expert scientists. I had worked daily, face to face with mental health patients providing group therapy sessions in an enclosed environment. I taught my patients effective coping skills to manage stress and anxiety during this time of severe crises in our world. I, too, was experiencing this crisis, feeling overwhelmed, giving so much of myself to my patients. The work environment was changing daily to keep up with the organization's and CDC safety guidelines. My body and mind felt pressured. It took extra effort for me to get to work every day. I had thoughts of decreasing my work hours but did not follow up or implement my plan.

I traveled to Eufaula more frequently to check on my mother, who was having physical problems with her knees requiring a medical procedure. I was with her to assist in her care at the beginning of this pandemic.

It was during this time in May 2020 when America was about to erupt like a volcano. Just as the lava gushes out of an erupted volcano, America began to erupt. America's race, health and economic disparities became center stage. Racial injustices, discrimination, police brutality, prejudices, biases, sexism, violence, unemployment and the plight of minorities came pouring out to the forefront.

America was experiencing civil unrest, becoming a nation dealing with one crisis after another. Just as a patient receiving therapy for pains of the past cannot heal until dealing with unresolved conflict from the past. America's unresolved conflicts of the past resurfaced to the present day in America as a result of the pandemic and civil unrest.

America began to experience and expose the history of pain, showing her true colors. The hidden agenda of the leadership was exposed for the world to see. Our government leaders turned our health crisis into a political movement. Americans' health, safety and wellbeing were placed second to political motivations.

Unfortunately, if a crisis is not resolved, it will show up, creating more chaos again, just as we are experiencing now in this country. America is broken, in pain, in chaos suffering from illnesses of the past being resurrected in the present.

On May 25, 2020, civil unrest erupted when George Floyd, an African American male, was killed by a white police officer putting his knee on his neck for eight minutes and forty-six seconds. It was recorded live on a video by someone standing by watching and begging the police officer to get off his neck. Not only were bystanders asking the policeman to get off George Floyd's neck, but George Floyd himself was also begging for his life, asking the officer to get off his neck, stating, "I can't breathe."

Watching the video caused me, and I believe many other people watching it, to be traumatized. Hearing a man beg for his life, watching the white police officer proudly putting extreme pressure with his knee squeezing the life from a human being for the entire world to see, was horrifying. In my mind, I wondered if seeing this televised murder of another human was comparable to what was experienced during slavery time when a slave was beaten, hung in front of or taken away from his family and other slaves.

I can imagine the terror they must have felt witnessing the degradation of another human being that way. I really did not want to believe we were at this point in American history where we are in an unprecedented global pandemic crisis, now the exposure of surgent racial discrimination, injustices and police brutality. It was unbelievable and difficult to digest. I struggled daily after seeing the video on television.

I also watched one of George Floyd's funeral services, where a civil rights activist preached the eulogy. He asked everyone in the church and those watching the televised services to stand up for the exact time the policemen had his knee on Mr. Floyd's neck. By the fourth minute, I lost it. I cried because I have never witnessed a human being treated in such an inhumane way. I felt angry, sad and defeated. I felt a sense of helplessness I have never experienced. I feared for the lives of all African American males, especially my two sons. I feared for myself and other African American females as well.

I had thoughts of how systemic racism has impacted the lives of African Americans in this country. I was angry and furious. I started thinking we should rename this country "Ameriterror" instead of America. "Ameriterror" is defined by me as a state of living in terror in America where American citizens are terrorized by people who are supposed to protect them. American has not been the land of the free and home of the brave for African Americans.

It felt like African Americans were being terrorized by law enforcement officers. African Americans have been treated unfairly since arriving in the country some 400 years ago as slaves. Not only did we have to deal with this COVID -19 pandemic, now I felt fearful for all people of color's lives. I felt like we were living in a third-world country where military and/or law enforcement people almost daily killed their own people. It felt like we were in a war zone, not the land of milk and honey.

My sentiments of racial discrimination were shared by many people who began protesting domestically and abroad after the world saw on a live-streamed video of how a white police officer felt bold enough to proudly put his knee on a black man's neck for all those minutes in front of witnesses in broad daylight with no compassion or care about killing a begging man who was pleading for his life.

This COVID-19 pandemic seemed to bring the worst out of law enforcement officers who were supposed to protect its citizens. There was a rise in policemen killing more black people, especially the males. It felt unsafe to go outside my home. I was concerned about my own sons. I talked to them daily, trying to prepare them for what was happening, expressing my fears for our lives. My youngest son did not share my sentiments. He stated he was not afraid and would not be scared to live his life. At the time, I had enough fear for us both.

I know being a Christian, I am not to fear the things of this world but too much was going on in America. I felt so hopeless because the country was out of control. It appeared as if another unarmed African American male was getting shot every week. There were increasing protests, riots surfacing throughout the country and abroad. The nightly news reported blasting imagery of buildings being burned, cars set afire and stores being looted. It appeared the volcano had erupted. Nothing felt like America was one of the most civilized countries in the world.

I was stopped by the police days after George Floyd's incident. I was afraid I would not make it back home alive. I was afraid of the people whose job was to protect me and others from violence. Our country was in an uproar because some law enforcement officers were killing unarmed citizens, what seemed like a weekly occurrence during this pandemic.

Changes were taking place in work environments where essential workers and first responders put their own lives in danger of being exposed to the virus while performing job duties. All work environments were making daily changes to maintain compliance with CDC and organizational guidelines to protect, prevent staff and consumers of services from COVID-19.

The Black Lives Matter movement was empowered, building rapidly domestically and internationally. The protesters were mostly young millennials leading the way. This time there were more white participants compared to the protesters of the 1960s. All races took to the streets to stand up for equal justice for all citizens in the United States. They took a stand to show the world black lives matter.

Changes in Schools and Colleges

Colleges and school systems shut down to protect students and staff during the beginning of the pandemic. Children were home all day, not attending school during the first few months after the virus spread rapidly throughout the country. Students began viral learning from home on social media when the schools reopened in the fall. As the school system and colleges began to reopen in the Fall, there was a surge in the number of coronavirus cases.

The news reported a situation where students attending one of the Universities in Alabama had a coronavirus party to see how many would become infected. They reportedly invited students with COVID-19 to the party, put money in a pot, and the one who became infected first received the pot of cash. This was an indication some of the younger people, college students specifically, were not taking this virus seriously. It appeared they were playing Russian roulette with their lives because people were dying at an enormous rate from COVID-19. They reportedly attended the party, failing to abide by the CDCs guidelines of wearing facial masks and staying six feet distances away from each other.

The country has been polarized about following the CDC's guidelines of wearing a mask. Some Citizens refused to wear a mask, stating it violates their rights of self-expression. Some stated they would not allow the government to dictate how they care for their health. Guidelines from the CDC were conflicting with what was being stated from our leadership at the white house. The president of the United States, many in his administration, and many of his followers refused to wear a mask for months until he was infected by COVID-19 on October 3, 2020. The guideline states people should wear a mask to protect themselves and others from getting COVID-19. If a leader does not adhere to his own CDC's health guidelines, the entire country suffers because mixed messages are sent out into the world. There are many conflicting messages communicated from our country's leaders daily, which poses a health and safety crisis.

I admit I was feeling some kind of way, seeing how careless and lack of concern our leaders have for the American people's welfare. When our president was diagnosed with COVID-19, I heard people express mixed feelings about him. Many people wished him a speedy recovery. Even I wished him well. I did not want anyone to be sick and weak because of the virus or share my experience.

I was healed. Being sick and helpless increased my faith and dependence on God. It also allowed me to trust and depend on God more. I was transformed. I hoped the experience would transform our leader into a more concerned person who would care more about the needs of the American people and not continue using the health crisis as a political ploy. To say I was disappointed is an understatement.

I know there is a big discrepancy in the medical services the rich, middle class and poor people receive in this country. I realize our leader should receive the best of care. I agree they should. The average American exposed to or infected with COVID-19 was initially instructed to be quarantined for at least fourteen days, and later it was dropped down to ten.

Our leader went to the hospital on a Friday, reportedly infected with the virus. On Sunday, two days later was seen on television outside riding in the car with secret service men waving at some of his supporters. I wondered if he thought about the impact of exposing his staff to a deadly virus could possibly kill them or their family members. Again, I felt indifferent about the choices made by the leader of this country. I stayed quarantined for more than fourteen days at home. I did not allow anyone inside my home because I did not want to infect or spread the virus. In fact, after having two positive tests following my initial test, I stayed home for another fourteen days. I followed the CDC guidelines because I cared about my family, friends and others. I did not want to expose them to the virus.

The media reported the president was discharged from Walter Reed Medical Center three days after reportedly being infected with the virus. Soon after returning to the white house, he was seen on television giving a thumbs up before walking inside. He was also seen on television taking off his mask, talking to news reporters standing beneath the balcony where he was standing.

I know he was given the best medications as the leader of our country. I propose that Congress pass a bill allowing every American infected by COVID-19 have access to the same medications he took while at Walter Reed Hospital. After all, it is the American people who pay for government official's medical treatment.

There media reported there have been numerous campaign rallies where the president has attended since stating he is cured and immune to COVID-19 after staying three days in Walter Reed Hospital. He has been observed not wearing a mask. The media reported he stated during one of his rallies that he could, "Kiss the pretty women and the men too."   I was shocked by this statement. Upon hearing his statement broadcasted on national television, I was experiencing COVID-19 impact over forty days since I was initially infected. I was just beginning to heal from a rash on my legs and arms from COVID 19. I remained cautious about being around people, let alone kiss someone.

I also heard our president say on National television, "I thank God I had COVID-19 and do not be afraid of it." I had COVID-19. I am telling everyone I know, "You do not want COVID-19. I do not want you to get it. Please be careful and be safe. Follow the CDC's health guidelines to protect yourself and others, and prevent the spread of the virus." No one knows what kind of impact the virus will have on their body and immune system. So many people have died, especially at the onset of this pandemic. The death rates continue to rise daily.

Many people in America and abroad are taking this virus very seriously. My family and I take the virus seriously, even more so after experiencing and being healed from it. Top scientists on the coronavirus task force encourage everyone to follow the CDC's guidelines to prevent the spread of the virus.

Changes In Shopping And Unemployment

The way we shopped changed. Some people shopped on the internet, having food and other items delivered to their homes. Others shopped for, food enduring waiting in long lines to purchase food and other needed items from local stores. Most of the local malls, shopping centers closed for safety reasons during the onset of the country's shutting down. It was mandated that only places that provided food and other necessary items remain open. Many other nonessential businesses were closed for weeks.

Many people became unemployed. America experienced the highest unemployment rate where the job market was destroyed by the global pandemic. The news reported the coronavirus made America's job market go from sixty to zero in the blink of an eye. Stay at home orders were issued by states to slow down the spread of the virus. The American economy was at a standstill. It was reported that over 58 million people initially applied for unemployment between March 2020 through August 2020. This was unprecedented, according to television news reports. Many families were barely surviving with unemployment compensation to provide for the needs of their families.

The coronavirus had such a significant spiraling impact on the American Economy. It felt like the worst natural disaster in our lifetime, especially with so many Americans dying of the virus. Our leaders were not prepared to handle a pandemic. America, one of the most civilized countries globally, lost so many lives because our country's leadership was seemingly unprepared to prevent and manage the pandemic.

Communication Changes

The way families communicated with extended relatives changed due to the health crisis of the global outbreak of COVID-19. Social media is being used to keep people connected, informed, safe and productive. Initially, families stayed home mostly except to pick up necessary items like food, gas, and medicines.

Most families communicate through social media or telephone because of fear of spreading or contracting the virus. Now we accept this pandemic as our "new normal." Many Americans are staying home and not leaving for any reason due to fear of being exposed to the virus. They are having food, clothes and other necessary items shipped or dropped off at their homes.

Many grocery stores and pharmacies are providing free home deliveries. Restaurants have grub hub services where orders are taken online and delivered to customers' homes.

I know a personal example of elderly people staying home because of fear of getting COVID-19. Some of my friends have encouraged me to shop from my home and not go out in public. There is fear the virus is airborne and can be transmitted if you go outside and breathe in the air. This is contrary to the CDC's finding. The virus is said to be airborne when an infected person breathes or sneezes into the air, then anyone within six feet can be exposed to the virus. In fact, the leading scientist has indicated it is better to have functions outside instead of inside where an infected person can expose others because the person infected is breathing into the air in an inside enclosed area.

There is a massive amount of information being shared about the coronavirus. The term "infodemic" is being used to describe an overload of information both on and offline. According to the World Health Organization, it includes misinformation used to undermine the public health response and advance alternative agendas of some groups or individuals. It can affect our physical as well as our mental health. Listening to misinformation can also create a health crisis, as is happening in the United States.

If our government had initially been transparent in advising Americans about the seriousness of the virus, followed the pandemic prevention plan outlined by the previous administration to prevent widespread exposure, the coronavirus would not have caused over two hundred thousand deaths between March 2020 and October 2020. The number of deaths continues to increase.

One of the ways I prevent an overload of information is by watching little television. At the beginning of this pandemic, I watched the news almost daily only to realize hearing negative news harmed my overall wellbeing. Listening to the news created fear and panic for me. I was always reading or listening to information about the coronavirus and of how law enforcement officers were shooting and killing unarmed black men. The news shared pictures of people being harassed, assaulted and killed by law enforcement officers. Some things should not be broadcasted because it creates chaos and fear among viewers. The reality is these types of incidents should not happen at all.

Every city where African American people were being killed by police incited peaceful protests, as well as riots, looting and violence. Within recent weeks, even peaceful protesters were killed, assaulted, or had tear gas sprayed on them at government law officials' orders. Unfortunately, peaceful protestors have been confronted with violence from other groups that do not believe in peaceful protest.

Social Media

Social media is keeping us safe because we can order food, clothing, medications and many other items online. These items can be shipped to our doorsteps. This prevents us from leaving our homes, hopefully staying safe. It can prevent us from being exposed to people outside of our homes, hopefully preventing exposure to the virus.

Medical Services

There are medical staff working away from home and maintaining their regular work schedule before and during the pandemic, placing themselves at a higher risk of being exposed and infected by the virus. They are very dedicated to caring for their patients. At the beginning of this pandemic, patients were dying in massive numbers alone in the hospitals. Family members were unable to visit sick relatives in the hospital dues to fear of the virus being spread. Nurses and other medical staff were there holding the hands of dying people who could not say their last goodbye to family members.

I was home alone initially when diagnosed with COVID-19. At first, I had thoughts of dying alone until I tapped into my faith. I realized God was with me throughout my illness, recovery and even now. I also did not want my mother to die alone in the hospital, where none of her family members were present with her. Watching the news and listening to the infodemics will impact your worldview tremendously. I stopped watching television, reading only the current events on my laptop or cell phone to stay abreast of updates on things I need to know about what was happening in our world.

Delivery of Services

The delivery of outpatient mental health and medical services have changed during this pandemic. Telehealth and Telemental health are very prevalent, being used to provide outpatient medical and mental health services. Instead of going into a doctor's office for medical or mental health services, it can be done on social media. Doctors, counselors, and therapists can consult, diagnose, and treat patients using smartphones, tablets, or computers. Face-to-face contact with medical providers was limited at the beginning of the shutdown due to the pandemic rapidly spreading throughout the country.

Also, going to see a doctor face to face required wearing a face mask with the patient's temperature being checked at the door by a nurse prior to coming inside the doctor's office. Someone who has tested positive for the virus was not being seen by most specialized doctors. Some doctors will not treat patients until a negative COVID-19 test result has been obtained to prevent the spread of the virus.

Since being diagnosed with COVID-19, I have rescheduled most of my yearly follow-up specialized doctor's visits until next year. I will not attend until I have a negative COVID-19 test result. I am still cautious about spreading the virus to others even after having no COVID-19 symptoms for over one month. I will wear a face mask and maintain my six feet distance from others who are not in my normal contact system.

Changes In Worship Services

Initially, when the country shut down, most of the Churches shut down as well. Even though most churches began having live-streamed services, it felt different than worshipping in the building fellowshipping with church members. Having personal face to face contact with fellow Christians was missing. I did not realize how important having fellowship with the saints was until it was taken away by this pandemic. I was able to stay connected by talking on the telephone and messaging on social media.

Going to church every Sunday has been part of my life since I was a little girl. My daddy was a Baptist preacher. I was a preacher's kid. I was expected to act like a Christian girl all the time. I literally thought I was supposed to be perfect, usually portraying the part. I was accustomed to being dressed up wearing coordinated colors with my clothing, high heel shoes as a teenager and young adult. My hairstyles were usually neat and nicely cut.

This perception followed me throughout my adult life. I liked the attention I felt standing out gaining compliments from family and friends. It was a privilege to afford the current fashions to look perfect. I always thought I should dress to impress. I know the way we look on the outside is irrelevant to what God sees on the inside. Our outer appearance has nothing to do with the way God sees us. The older I became, I realized God looks at the inside of a person's heart and not the outer appearance.

I also grew up attending Sunday School, where children were taught the BIBLE (Basic Instructions before leaving earth). Over the years, Sunday School seems to have phased out of the church. I believe the lack of Bible teachings and training has contributed to the demise of our societal values and morals about spirituality. I have always been an active, faithful participant in my church. I was a Sunday School teacher, choir member and worked as coordinator of the Church's Youth Department when I attended Church while living at home as a teenager and young adult. I am active in the Church I currently attend. I serve as a Greeter Team Leader, Co-Chair of the Education Ministry and serve on the Service Ministry, preparing the communion table before Church services start during my assigned time.

Attending Church services worshipping God has been part of my life for as long as I can remember. At age two or three years old, my mother would awaken my four siblings and me early on Sunday mornings to eat a cooked breakfast, dressed us for Sunday School with coordinating clothes, lace socks, and black patent leather shoes. It felt good dressing up for Church services. We teased our brothers, saying they were wearing their "Sunday going to meeting" suits.

She would put an extra effort into buying Easter clothes to wear to

Church on Easter Sunday. For some reason, as a little girl, it seemed like the church pews were filled with people wearing new clothes on holidays such as Easter and Christmas. As I get older, I've noticed people do not seem to attend Church as much as we did when I was growing up. Also, back then, it seemed as if we stayed at church all day long. My siblings and I did not complain because my father was a preacher. He was there all day long, every Sunday almost. I took those values about Church into my adulthood. I brought my two sons up in church, making sure they received biblical teachings and training. They attended every Sunday with me.

This pandemic has revealed new awareness for me. I miss seeing, having worship and fellowship with my sisters and brothers in Christ.

However, since being infected and healed from COVID- 19, I have a more intimate relationship with God. I have been transformed into a higher spiritual growth. My spirituality, worshipping God in spirit and truth, has grown beyond measure. I am more aware as I experience God's presence in my life throughout my days now. I have more conversations and talks with Him. My prayer life has increased to become more meaningful. I read the Bible more. I think more about his words daily. I share His blessings with others daily.

His faithfulness to my family and me is unmeasurable. I praise God more for his goodness, mercy and favor. Every time I see a clear blue sky, the sunshine or feel the wind blowing across my skin, l appreciate His beautiful creation more. Hearing the birds sing every morning is music to my ears. Now, I take time to smell the roses, honeysuckles, daisies, or flowers within close proximity.

A daily walk and talk with God maintain my spiritual health and growth. I am growing in altruism, focusing on how I can help and serve others. I practice the principle of living to give and not living to get. I know there is a higher calling on my life than serving my own selfish needs. Christians are called to be Christ-like, to love our neighbor as we love ourselves. I consider myself a servant of God. Serving God means serving His people. I enjoy serving others.

Historically, the black church played a pivotal role in the black community as a safe haven to worship God. It was also a place dedicated to building up the African American Community. The coronavirus pandemic caught all of us off guard, including the Black Church. During this pandemic, some churches have failed to meet the congregations and communities' needs at large. There has been a lack of outreach in assisting parishioners with preventive measures to assist in protecting themselves from contracting COVID-19.

Some churches have failed to give out protective and preventive supplies such as masks, gloves, and sanitary supplies to prevent the spread of the virus. Many of the churches are not having regular on-site service. Many are having services lived stream on Facebook or Zoom. They are collecting tithes as if the members are still attending. Many have closed the doors to prevent the spread of the virus. Community outreach has suffered as a result of the pandemic.

I remember church people having genuine care and concern about each other's plight back in the days when I was a child growing up. This pandemic apparently has caused a disconnect between church members because of being quarantined, fear of catching the virus, and understandably so. Maybe I am expecting more than the church can give since this pandemic caught us unprepared.

We are all still making the best of this unprecedented experience. I am praying, and I believe we will come back better. We will evaluate changes to be made within ourselves and our churches to hopefully be more prepared in the future. We will pick up the pieces, learn the lessons, look at the blessings and move forward to our new normalcy.

Changes in Voting

This is a presidential election year with much chaos in this country. There are voter suppression schemes to keep the American people from exercising their right to vote. Some leaders are especially trying to suppress the African Americans vote because when we stand together as a race of people, we become powerful. We can bring about a positive change in our government.

In 1870, the 15th Amendment gave African Americans the right to vote. Many innocent people sacrificed their lives, leading to African Americans exercising the right to vote. We will not stand around, allowing anyone to steal our votes and use scare tactics to prevent us from voting. We are taking souls to the polls this year. We will show up in massive numbers to show our ancestors their sacrifices were not in vain.

The way we vote has changed during this pandemic. To protect ourselves and others from being exposed to or infected by COVID-19, we are mandated to wear masks covering our nose, mouth and asked to maintain six feet distance away from others who are not a part of our immediate family.

The media reported this election year has posed difficulties with absentee or mail-in votes due to the government making critical changes to debunk the United States Post Office by removing public collection boxes to prevent voters from sending in early ballots. This became one of many national scandals used by our government to suppress voting in what has been described by the media as one of the most crucial presidential elections we have experienced in this country's history.

This pandemic alone posed difficulties in getting absentee votes to the county election offices throughout the United States. People were somewhat fearful of mailing their votes, afraid they would not reach the desired destination due to reports of some postal workers tampering with ballots by throwing them in the trash or burning ballots. This caused the mobilization of voters in massive numbers going to the county election office in person to complete absentee ballots instead of mailing in the ballots.

Also, all voters were encouraged by local officials to vote early to prevent having to stand in long lines during the general election on November third of this year. The pandemic also allowed more people to vote early due to the health crisis as a preventive measure to limit the number of people and length of time standing in line on election day. This plan proved beneficial because voters have turned out in record numbers to prevent experiencing what is predicted to be a chaotic election day this year. It was predicted that one hundred million voters would vote early, completing absentee voting ballots.

I completed the application and voted absentee for the first time since casting my first vote over forty years ago. It was a pleasant experience without chaos and confusion. I felt safer with fewer people attending. The county staff members were patient and helpful. It was an empowering experience casting my vote in this crucial presidential election. I realize one vote does matter because, with my vote, I expressed my voice. I encouraged my family, friends, associates and others to exercise their hard-earned right to vote. This election will determine if our leader in chief, the president of the United States, will be someone who will put the needs of the American people first and foremost.

There have been many unbelievable changes made by the current administration, which has manifested more racial division, outward expressions of violence, discriminations against minorities by law enforcement officers and random whites who claim to be supreme to other races. At times it feels as if we are headed to a racial and another civil war here in America. This pandemic pushed more voters to turn out early to speak their voice during this election year.

I will admit the human part of me feels concerned about this year's election outcome due to the pandemic. I am concerned the myriad of political changes, scare tactics and unresolved issues we face in America will continue to erupt. I am concerned this virus has not and will not be contained if changes are not made, which will cause more Americans to be exposed, infected and die.

This fall, we are experiencing a surge in COVID-19 cases. I am concerned the poverty level for minorities will increase. The health and economic disparities will widen as the rich continue to get richer, and the middle class becomes poor. It is evident as the fortunes of the billionaire have doubled or tripled during this pandemic while those who are unemployed are living beneath the poverty level, trying to feed families on a small portion of funds they receive from unemployment compensation.

We must continue to trust God to bring us through this difficult time in our lives. I have tapped into my faith daily to ask God for guidance to remove my fears. I trust God to bring us out of the worst American crisis of my lifetime. I will practice what I have preached to my patients and clients over the years using coping strategies to manage during a crisis, which is our Goliath, the COVID-19 pandemic.

Chapter 7
Coping strategies to manage changes during Pandemic

L iving each day to deal with changes during this pandemic has been challenging. Having a survival plan with coping strategies has been helpful to manage during this crisis. Listed below are coping strategies to use to make this crisis more manageable.

1. Believe the pandemic will end.

Nothing lasts forever except for the presence of God in our lives. One of my favorite quotes by Robert H. Schuller is, "Tough times never last. Tough people do." There is nothing new under the sun. One day this pandemic will end. I believe this to be true, just like the flu was a pandemic when it arrived on the scene in. A vaccine was developed and widely used in the United

States beginning. It took time to come up with a vaccine.

In today's world, some brilliant scientists and chemists are working on discovering a vaccine for COVID-19 with God's help. This virus, like the influenza virus, will stay around, but a vaccine will be developed to prevent its spread. Believe and expect good results to come forth. Trust God to deliver us from this crisis. He can work a miracle if He desires. Even if God does not cure it today, I know God is able. He can do anything but fail. His timing is perfect. His deliverance will be on time, according to His will. He worked a miracle in my family by healing all of us from COVID-19. I praise and honor God for his favor, grace, and mercy given to my family and me.

2. Tap into your faith and believe God will bring you out better than before

Continue worshipping God in Spirit and Truth throughout this pandemic. Read your Bible. Look at all the catastrophes and plagues encountered by people in the old testament. Our faith tells us we should believe good things will come even when we do not see them in front of our faces. This pandemic is a scary time. It is something we have never experienced before in our lifetime. Christians are not expected to worry. Life is difficult with all the challenges confronting us during this pandemic. We must choose our faith over fear. "Without faith, it is impossible to please God." Tapping into your faith is the best strategy a Christian can use when dealing with difficulties in life.

I know I could not have survived my COVID-19 experience without tapping into my faith. I asked God to strengthen my faith when I was sick. I asked God to heal my family and me. He did because my faith was activated. I started believing we would be better each day, and we did.

I am a living testimony. I am better than I was before because of my faith and trust in God. I am a more mature Christian because of my COVID-19 experience. I am no longer afraid, anxious and overwhelmed by the crisis situations going on in our country. I know those battles are not mine to fight. I gave my burdens to God, who can carry them. I released them from my shoulders. I was able to "Let go and let God" handle them.

3. Use the coping skills that worked for you in the past

This pandemic is a great time to reflect on the coping skills you used to manage a crisis in the past. Think about how you handled the last crisis you experienced. Hindsight is 2020. Use what was effective in helping you overcome the situation that seemed unbearable to you. You are still alive. You survived it. Think about how you made it over. When we overcome a crisis, we learn lessons on how to survive the next one. Our experiences prepare us for new things on the horizon.

Think back and make a list of the coping skills used in the past. Make sure your list includes positive and effective coping skills. Sometimes when overwhelmed, people will relapse back to ineffective ways of coping to get a quick fix or try to escape reality. Most of the time, using ineffective coping skills will lead to future problems.

Many people will revert to addictive behaviors such as using drugs, alcohol, gambling and other behaviors. These behaviors will give a quick fix or a quick escape. They will also compound current problems leading to more chaos and confusion. Be proactive. Make a list of effective positive coping skills used in the past.

4. Maintain daily contact with others while in isolation

This pandemic has presented a huge social isolation problem, especially for people like me who live alone. Isolation for long periods can present mental health problems like depression. People who are severely depressed will isolate to prevent social contact with others. It is important to talk to someone daily on the phone or using social media. Maintain contact with others to let them know how you are managing this new way of living. Share your feelings and concerns with others. You will learn other people share similar feelings and concerns. You will not feel alone, as if you are the only person experiencing certain fears or feelings. It can be a scary time for all of us. Stay connected to God, your power source, family and friends.

5. Find ways to prevent Depression while Isolating.

Go outside and experience God's creation

This pandemic has caused stress, anxiety and could lead to depression. One of the symptoms of depression is isolation. In this pandemic, having to isolate from others can cause the onset of a depressive episode. If you feel depressed while isolating, please seek help from a licensed counselor, therapist or psychologist.

One of my favorite morning rituals is to go outside, sit in my patio area to experience God's creation. I love listening to the birds singing in the trees. I love to look up into the pretty blue sky even if dark clouds are present. Just being outside allows me to experience nature, God's beautiful creation. I feel alive and rejuvenated when I feel the morning breeze while breathing in the fresh air.

Learn to appreciate the simple things in life. Sit outside if you can.

Drink a cup of coffee, tea, a glass of fresh orange juice, a glass of water or whatever you prefer. If unable to sit outside, look outside a window to see God's creation. Dream about being on the beach or at your favorite place. Find your own ways to prevent depression while isolating during this pandemic.

7. Find A reason to Celebrate Each Day

Look for a reason to celebrate each day. Waking up, getting out of bed and starting each new day is a reason to celebrate. Being alive is a great reason to celebrate. Some people did not awaken to see a new day.

I praise God every day for allowing me to live and not die. Over one million people throughout the world have already died during this pandemic. The United States has experienced more deaths than any other country in the world. If you are reading this book, you are alive. Celebrate being alive. Celebrate love. Celebrate you.

Find a reason to celebrate each day. It does not have to be a major celebration. It could be just a simple smile when you wake up. Look at yourself in the mirror and say to yourself, "I am still alive. It is going to be a great day." Praise God by giving thanks for allowing you to see another new day.

8. Make A gratitude list every morning

Making a gratitude list gives you something good to think about at the beginning of your day. It allows you to look at what is good or what you can look forward to during your day. Practice writing down why you are grateful. Be glad it happened or will happen.

One day as I was traveling to work on the Boulevard, I passed several traffic lights. All the lights were green as I was passing through. When I arrived at my desk, I put it down on my gratitude list. I was grateful for all the green lights. I made it to work on time. I felt grateful the traffic lights were not on red.

Our gratitude list should include something different every day. Once I heard a speaker say our level of happiness will improve if we make a gratitude list of five things each day.

He suggested writing a gratitude list for 21 days would lead to a habit. I tried it for 21 days, and it became a habit. I am a living testimonial of making a daily gratitude list increased my overall level of happiness. It sets the mood for a good day by focusing on what is good in life.

Practice making a gratitude list to improve your level of happiness. It works. Any plan will work if you work it. You may need to change a plan but keep working on it until you find positive results.

9. Pray for self, others, healing and world peace

Praying is my way of communicating my needs to God. He already knows my needs but requires me to take a step in activating my faith in Him. Pray daily without ceasing. Pray for yourself, family, friends, enemies, healing and world peace. Pray for healing in our land. Pray for God to heal the land of COVID-19.

10. Journal Your thoughts about the pandemic

Writing or journaling your thoughts, feelings and mood is a good stress reliever. It is also therapeutic. It allows an opportunity to get things out of your mind onto paper. It allows an opportunity to reflect on what you have written to change your perspective or worldview about a situation.

Journaling can give a snapshot of the changes needed. It can be used as a goal-setting tool to bring goals and visions into focus. It can serve as a reminder of the growth achieved from one day to the next. Journaling is a record of the present to be viewed in the future. It can be a tool used to document your thoughts about the pandemic and other situations you experience daily. It is your legacy of the past when read in the future to come.

11. Maintain A Daily Routine

Develop a daily routine to maintain a sense of normalcy during this pandemic. Our old life has passed and gone. Develop your new normal way of existing during this pandemic. Develop a daily routine conducive to growth and development. Develop a new mindset to maintain your sanity. As I stated earlier, my sanity has been compromised during this pandemic. Watching the video of a human being killed by a police officer was traumatizing for me. I am still working on maintaining my sanity.

Like recovery, it is ongoing.

12. Exercise Daily

Exercise daily to maintain mental and physical health. Exercise also helps to maintain a healthy weight. Many of my friends have expressed what they describe as "Quarantine weight gain" due to social isolation and unhealthy eating habits. Exercise can help control undesirable weight gain during the pandemic. Exercise at least 30 minutes daily. Use exercise equipment, walk, dance or do aerobic exercises. It will also reduce stress and anxiety associated with changes due to the pandemic.

Develop your own exercise plan.

13. Eat Healthy

Eating healthy is essential to a healthy body and mindset. Top Scientists list having a healthy diet with nutritious eating habits is one of the main keys to maintaining a healthy immune system. During this pandemic, it is essential to have a healthy immune system to prevent and/or fight the coronavirus. Eat healthy foods limiting unhealthy snacking. It is easy to get off track with all the changes faced during this pandemic.

Maintain healthy eating habits throughout this pandemic.

It was difficult for me to maintain a healthy diet throughout my COVID-19 experience. I struggled with eating proper foods while sick with the virus. I lost my sense of taste and smell during the first week. I did not fully regain my taste and smell until one month after being infected. Once my taste returned, I was eating foods with less nutritional value. It has been a struggle to get back on track with healthy eating habits.

14: Get Proper Sleep

My sleep pattern has been disrupted since being infected with COVID-19. I was accustomed to getting eight or more hours of sleep each night before getting sick with the virus. Since being infected, it is difficult to sleep eight hours. It is usually five to seven hours most days now.

Proper sleep is essential to good health. The health experts recommend seven to eight hours daily. The top scientist on the Pandemic Task Force stated getting proper sleep is essential for a healthy immune system. Sleep is restorative. It involves healing and repairing our body.

Having a daily sleep regimen can be helpful. It is a good idea to go to bed at the same time each night and awaken at the same time each morning to develop healthy sleep patterns. A good night's sleep is a good remedy to start a good day.

Taking a nap during the day can also be beneficial during this pandemic. It can be a brief escape. It can also make you feel rejuvenated, giving you the energy to complete daily tasks.

15. Celebrate Your Accomplishments

Often when I am preparing to move forward in my life, I reflect on my achievements. I will look at my accomplishments. I will place my greatest accomplishments in front of my face on or around my desk area. It gives me the motivation to move forward.

We have all accomplished something in our lives. Celebrate what you have already accomplished. Have a "Celebrate me" day. You are designed by God. You are special. We are all surviving during this pandemic. It is not an easy task. The pandemic brought many changes and challenges.

I am grateful God gave me the strength and courage to change my perceptions about what I was experiencing as a result of this Pandemic and other world chaos. I celebrate being transformed from feeling overwhelmed with stress and anxiety. I celebrate being alive; every morning, I awaken.

16. Dream Big and Set New Goals

Many people are realizing new gifts and talents during this pandemic. It is a great opportunity to dream big, set new or strive to meet unmet goals. Have a purpose-driven life. Ask God to give you a new vision. It is during our most difficult times we realize our true strength and endurance. Be like our presidential candidate who states he wants to "Build back better." Build yourself better during this pandemic.

17. Complete A Vision Board

As you are dreaming for bigger and better complete a vision board. Write down your biggest and wildest dream on a vision board. This pandemic has taken away so many lives. It presents an urgency to live life to the fullest each day. Now is the time to ask for God's guidance in reaching higher heights to our goals. Dream big. Write your vision today.

Be creative with your vision board. Make it artful and colorful. Use a poster, cardboard, sheet of paper, piece of cloth or whatever you prefer to make a vision board. Once you have completed your vision board, place it where you can see it throughout your day to remind you to keep dreaming. Then, take steps to reach one dream at a time until your visions become a reality.

18. Look for the good in all situations.

Smile at yourself for surviving up until now. We are resilient. We are survivors. We will bounce back better. Look for the good in all situations. There are lessons and blessings during this pandemic.

My blessings are unmeasurable. I surrendered my burdens to God during this pandemic. I learned I am unable to carry the weights of this world on my shoulders. I am blessed because I am no longer stressed, anxious or afraid. I live a carefree and peaceful life despite the turmoil going on around me. Every day I look at the good things God has done in my life.

19. Praise God for all Blessings

I am so grateful God is preeminent in my life. I could not survive this pandemic or any other crisis in my life without God. I will continually keep praise in my heart and on my lip because of the goodness of my God. When I felt alone during this pandemic, God showed how He is always with me. His presence surrounds me. I have learned to count and praise God for all blessings. I have learned to praise God for what I perceived as the small things in my life. I have reframed my thinking to see even the small things are a big deal to give God praise.

Focusing on the negative impact of this pandemic will create stress and anxiety in our lives. We must focus on what is good in our lives despite this pandemic. God's presence is my saving grace. Without my God, I am nothing. The saying goes, "When the praises go up, the blessings will rain down." Praise God from your hearts, being grateful for all blessings. When we send up praises, God will cause blessings to rain down upon us. There is no greater reward than to feel a shower of God's blessings coming down upon us.

Give God praise during this pandemic. Do a praise dance. Get a shout on if you like. However, get your praise on. Choose to praise God. Do it daily throughout this pandemic.

The Serenity Prayer

"God grant me the serenity to accept the things I cannot change, courage to change the things I can and wisdom to know the difference." Reinhold Niebuhr

Chapter 8
Positive Changes to make during the pandemic

———————————o———————————

An unprecedented pandemic along with uprising racial tension, increase in violence, social injustices, discrimination and police brutality aimed at African Americans, people dying daily from COVID-19, and homes being destroyed by wildfires all happening simultaneously can feel as if the world may be coming to an end. It can make you feel as if you have no control. It makes you feel like the world is out of control. It can also create fear and cause you to operate in panic mode. It can create insurmountable stress and anxiety in life. It makes you think life is one big crisis after another. At times it may cause you to think, "I can't make it one more day in this chaotic world." I have good news to reveal to you. You can and you will survive the chaos we now experience as we face the pandemic at this juncture in our lives.

We are survivors. We are resilient. We can, and we will bounce back stronger than ever before. Our faith will carry us through these trials and tests. God will help us when we ask Him to help us bear our burdens. We cannot do it alone. All things are possible with God. He has brought us through many impossibilities we would have never imagined we could overcome had we continued looking at our problems through our worldly eyes. Change your worldview to seeing burdens through spiritual eyes.

God will never fail or forsake us. He will use our burdens as a test of our faith to bring us closer to Him. Unfortunately, the world has become focused on greed and not our God. He is our alfa and omega. Our beginning and our end. America was built on spiritual principles but has changed vision over the years leading to the demise of moral, spiritual and innate character. America requires change. The change can start within each one of us. God commanded in the scripture, "That ye love one another, even as I have loved you." We can change how we treat each other. We can treat others the way we want to be treated with dignity and respect.

One of the ten commandments states, "Thou shall have no other God before me." Until we get our lives in order with God's plan, we will continue to drift like a ship tossed back and forth in the waters. We will have no peace in our lives. We will feel lost and out of control in this sinful world.

There are changes we can make to regain a sense of control during this pandemic and turmoil we are experiencing in our world today. First, we must put God at the center of our lives. We must love nothing more than we love God, our power source. We must trust God to bring us out of this pandemic better than we were before it happened. As a Christian, I believe God has my best interest in mind, even when confronted with a major life crisis. There is always a lesson to learn, even if we cannot immediately see the purpose from the beginning.

Sometimes we complete the journey before we know the lesson behind the test or trials we experienced. I had no idea my lesson from being sick with COVID-19 was to transform me into a stronger believer in God. I believed my faith was strong before the sickness. I had to go through the test to really know and understand the power of God's presence in my life. I realized my focus was diverted by what appeared to be insurmountable crisis situations instead of focusing on my God, who could calm the roaring seas.

I was like Peter walking on water in the scriptures of Matthew 14:30, "But when he saw the wind was boisterous, he was afraid and beginning to sink he cried out, saying, Lord save me." I was focusing on the problems and not the problem solver. I knew I was unable to solve the problems going on in this world. My shoulders were not big enough to carry those burdens. I felt powerless until I was able to put things into the proper perspective by giving them to God, who can bear all things. The burdens of this world were impossible for me to bear alone.

It appeared as if every day brought on a new crisis. The television news reported and sensationalized another tragedy every day. It was disturbing, creating more anxiety and stress the more I watched the news. I had to make a change to discontinue watching the daily news to protect my own mental health. When we inundate our minds with negative stimuli, we will reinforce negative responses in our lives. It will affect our health mentally, physically and spiritually.

When America saw how George Floyd was killed by the policemen, it triggered a response. Many Americans responded by protesting, rioting and looting. Americans were on edge. They wanted to see a change in the way police officers responded to citizens. The Black Lives Matter Movement erupted and began a peaceful protest in almost every city in the United States and abroad. Changes were necessary. Change is often met with resistance. To grow and become a better country, America must make changes. To become a stronger Christian, we must make changes in our life. Changes are not always comfortable. Sometimes we go through many difficulties to get to where we are destined to be.

One of the most powerful changes we can make daily is to evaluate our thought process. We can evaluate how what we think affects us. When awakening in the morning, examine what you are thinking about your day. Decide if it is a positive or negative thought. If it is positive, you can continue thinking positively and have a great day.

However, if you awaken with negative thinking, you have the power to change it. Our thoughts are powerful and control our world. The Bible says in Proverbs 23, "As a man thinketh in his heart, so is he."

My thoughts about this pandemic, being sick with the virus changed after I was infected with it. Prior to being sick, I was afraid of being exposed, infected and believed I would die if I got it. When I was infected, I was afraid for myself and my family initially. I had to change my own perception about my situation. I know from experience thoughts are powerful and can control how you feel and act. I had to confront my illness face to face. I tapped into my faith, believing my family and I would be healed. If I had continued thinking negative, the results would have been different.

The lesson learned from my experience was the result of the changes I made early on during my COVID-19 experience.

We can change our attitude during this pandemic. Have an attitude of gratitude. Complaining about the pandemic does not bring about positive change. It creates more negative energy. Only God can change the pandemic and our perception about it. We can practice using coping skills to manage how we handle the changes brought on by the pandemic.

Our survival depends on our attitude. A good attitude helps us live our best life. A bad attitude keeps us stagnated. We will not grow or prosper with a bad attitude to life. We learned in elementary school how our attitude determines our altitude in life. Be positive. Be optimistic. Keep a good attitude, and you will be better when the pandemic is over.

Lastly and most importantly, we can change from focusing on fear to tapping into our faith. At the beginning of the pandemic, I was focusing on my fears of catching the virus. I was living in panic mode, creating undue stress and anxiety. I felt overwhelmed. I felt hopeless. I was afraid of dying when I was infected with the virus. When I became ill from the virus, I was at my lowest point. I was unable to care for myself. God stepped in to carry me when I could not carry myself.

My faith was tested and stretched. The human side of me was afraid. The spiritual side of me began to fight for me. My faith connected me with God, my power source. My life began to change when I surrendered myself to God.

Choose faith over fear. Tap into your spiritual power source. You and God makes a majority. No weapon formed against you will prosper. You will win the battle with God on your side.

But grow in the grace and knowledge of our Lord and Savior Jesus Christ. To him, be the glory both now and forever. Amen. 2 Peter 3:18

Chapter 9
Personal Growth During Pandemic

I have grown tremendously during this quiet meditative period of my life. I have experienced introspection, soul searching, nurtured myself and identified my purpose for this juncture in my life. I am at peace, feeling an unspeakable joy I have never experienced in my life. Life is good, easy and beautiful. I love myself more than I have in the past. I have time to take care of me, being true to who I am becoming with God leading the way.

As a young adult, I made decisions that lead me down some roads I should not have taken. Now, as a mature adult, I know I cannot grow if there are no mistakes, failures and flops along the way. Today, I think about some of the things I thought I wanted or had to have in my life in my past. I did not know any better back then. I am so grateful God did not give me what I thought I desperately needed or wanted as a young adult. Praise God for knowing my future because I could only see the present at the time. I saw my life through rose-colored glasses. I could not see beyond what I was experiencing at that moment. I have a clearer vision. I once thought 20/20 vision was the best to have. Now, during the year 2020, with the country's turmoil, dealing with the pandemic and racial injustices, I believe it is clear my personal growth has given me a clearer vision. I see clearly through my spiritual eyes with my God leading the way. Without God, I am nothing.

I have told myself and some of my friends, "Self- preservation should be number one in our life." As I am aging, I am taking better care of my physical, mental and spiritual health. I practice thinking positive, being optimistic and looking for the good things in my life daily. I live in expectancy of good things happening. I have learned we usually get what we expect. When bad things happen, I started looking for the good in bad situations. All situations have lessons and blessings when we look for them.

This pandemic has presented one of the greatest health scares for my family and me when we were infected. It is by God's grace we are still alive. He worked miracles in our lives. We are all still alive by His grace.

The pandemic brought out America's brokenness to the surface. Unfortunately, many lives were lost due to the virus and the violence taking place in America. I have always said there will be blessings with some good things happening as a result of this pandemic. I believe positive changes are on the way. Historically, before a change came to the American system of injustice, racial discrimination and degradation of a people, there were sacrifices made. America is changing, and I expect positive changes will happen after the turmoil is over.

Hopefully, one day American will rise up to the creed of being the land of the free and home of the brave for all American citizens and not a select few. One day I believe America will treat citizens non-discriminately like with the pandemic. The coronavirus does not care about ethnicity, income, sex, education, social status, or other demographics. It has hit across the board. The impact has been more severe among people of color due to disparities in health care and income.

I am more optimistic about positive changes happening in America. My spiritual growth manifested a new hope and belief in God. I believe God wants His children, not a select few, to be treated equally and prosper. God will, for our lives, be done. I am living in expectancy for greater things to come.

Chapter 10
Conclusion

M y COVID-19 illness journey lasted sixty days. I am healed from the virus after having four positive test results from the onset to the end of having the infection. My COVID-19 test results on day # 60 came back negative. I felt relieved with a sense of freedom, knowing the virus was no longer present in my body. I also realize there may be residual effects from COVID-19, which may present later symptoms.

God answered my prayer of protection for all my organs. None were damaged, to my knowledge. I experienced no breathing difficulties. I am not boasting, but thankful for my outcome. I realize this virus can be fatal. The fatalities are rising as I am writing these words. Over one million lives have been reportedly taken worldwide due to COVID-19, with a prediction of more deaths to come as the surge in cases continues during the cold and flu season.

During my personal experience, I wondered why my family members received negative results after 14 days while I received a negative test after sixty days. I realized I was again being tested by COVID-19. I constantly reminded my giant of COVID-19 that my God was more powerful. I realized my strength in God. I maintained my optimistic attitude throughout the 60 days because I knew God was still with me. I claimed healing and victory. I told COVID-19, "I am winning."

I am blessed beyond measure to share my family's COVID-19 experience. My purpose is to offer hope and encouragement during this pandemic. I shared my family's experience with COVID-19 as a testimony of the miracles God is working in our lives. I know it is a rarity for 10 members of the same family being infected at the same time with COVID-19, and all of them survive without the loss of life. God was on our side.

My testimony is knowing with God on our side, we can do all things. We are winning in this season regardless of the giants we are now facing in America. We have a guide to follow. The Bible was written for instruction and learning. There is nothing new under the sun. There were plagues, catastrophes, crises, challenges and giants experienced by our ancestors before we were born. They survived. We will survive as well with God leading the way.

Through my personal experience, my lesson learned was to lean solely on God to bring me through my illness. I learned to trust God at His word to take care of my family and me. He came through. The lesson for this world is to turn from wickedness back to God. We must let go of worshipping worldly things, lean on God to help us and heal this land.

While I was sick with COVID-19, I was concerned about getting well. My and my family's health was my main concern. I also wanted to make sure my soul was right with God, just in case I died during my illness. God has a greater purpose for my life.

God allowed me to live to give a testimony about His goodness. I have a new praise to share daily with others. I have a new hope to share. My life has a new meaning. I am spreading the good news as I share my COVID-19 experience with the world. I have been transformed into a stronger Christian who walks closely with God daily. My life's journey was changed during this pandemic. I focus on my faith and not fear. I am living my life on a higher level to please and worship my God. My life is a living testimony. To Almighty God, I give all the glory and praise. Again, I say to COVID-19, "Meet My God." Hallelujah! Hallelujah! Hallelujah!

Trust in the Lord with all thine heart; and lean not unto thine understanding. In all thy ways acknowledge him, and he shall direct thy paths. Be not wise in thine own eyes: fear the Lord and depart from evil. Proverbs 3:5-7

JOURNAL YOUR PANDEMIC 2020
REFLECTION NOTES

_____

_____

_____

_____

_____

_____

_____

_____

_____

_____

_____

_____

_____

_____

_____

_____

_____

_____

_____

List Positive Coping Skills you will use to Manage During This Pandemic

_____

_____

_____

_____

_____

_____

_____

_____

_____

_____

_____

_____

_____

_____

_____

_____

_____

_____

_____

List Changes you have made or plan to make during this pandemic

_____

_____

_____

_____

_____

_____

_____

_____

_____

_____

_____

_____

_____

_____

_____

_____

_____

_____

_____

_____

_____

Reflection Notes